Holding Down The Fort

The Military Spouse's Guide to Surviving and Thriving

By
Navenka Gabrielson

Holding Down The Fort - The Military Spouses Guide to Surviving and Thriving

Copyright © 2017 Navenka Jane Gabrielson

All rights reserved. No part of this book may be reproduced in any form or by any electronic or mechanical means, including information storage and retrieval systems, without permission in writing from the author. For information, contact Navenka Jane Gabrielson at www.bodyharmonyonline.com.

The content of this book is for general instruction only. Each person's physical, emotional, and spiritual condition is unique. The instruction in this book is not intended to replace or interrupt the reader's relationship with a physician or other professional. Please consult your doctor for matters pertaining to your specific health and diet.

The author's reference to specific brands does not equal endorsement or sponsorship.

© Integrative Nutrition Inc. Integrative Nutrition Inc. does not endorse the content contained in this book.

All rights reserved. No part of this publication may be reproduced, distributed, or transmitted in any form or by any means, including photocopying, recording, or other electronic or mechanical methods, without the prior written permission of the publisher or author, except in the case of brief quotations embodied in critical reviews and certain other noncommercial uses permitted by copyright law. For permission requests, email the author and send your request to navenka@bodyharmonyonline.com

To contact the publisher, visit www.bodyharmonyonline.com

To contact the author, visit www.bodyharmonyonline.com

ISBN-13: 978-0692970287
ISNB -10: 0692970282
Printed in the United States of America

Cover by Hoka Hey! thom@hokahey.agency
Back Cover Photo by Payge Brandt Photography

Dedication

To every military spouse - may you stay true to yourself, be strong, resilient, and open to new adventures throughout your military life.

Thank you for serving alongside your spouse.

Acknowledgements

Thank you to all my clients, you are amazing! The changes you make in your lives are incredibly inspiring. Watching you turn your lives around is rewarding and keeps me motivated. You inspired me to get out of my comfort zone to write this book.

Thank you to all of you who filled out surveys as part of my research. Thank you to all my beta readers for your ideas and helpful insights. Your thoughts shaped my ideas and turned them into this book.

Many thanks to my reviewers, friends, and family who gave their support and kept me on track during the writing process. To my children for your patience when mom spent hours typing during your summer break! A special shout-out to my brother Thomas Heap at Hoka Hey Graphic Design, who designed the cover, to Payge Brandt for the great photo shoot, to my editor, Krystal Boots, who was not only a great editor but someone who could relate to my book, her mother and grandmother being military spouses themselves. Knowing people believed in me spurred me on.

Lastly, to my husband: Without you, I would not be on this adventure. I am proud of you, and your service, and I am proud to be your wife. Thank you for believing in me, and for supporting everything I do.

Contents

Introduction 13
My Story

My Aha Moment
Peace at Last
How to Use this Book

Chapter 1 25
Who Am I?

Client Testimony
Your Life Is Happening Now.
Is it Making you Happy?
Take Action!
The Scenario
Bucket List Goals
What Do I Want?
The Million Dollar Question!
Exercise 1 - What Do I Want?
Client Story
Client Story
Exercise 2 - Making Your Gut Instinct List
Exercise 3 - Build Your Mind Map

Chapter 2 59
Connection

Your Relationship with Yourself…
Exercise 4 - Let's Love Ourselves Up!
Exercise 5 - What You Like About Me
Exercise 6 - Who Am I?
Exercise 7 - A Deeper Internal Look
Exercise 8 - Playful Me!
Exercise 9 - Mind Map Connections
Building your Independence Muscle!
Pressing the Pause Button on Life

Financial Independence
Client Story
Your Relationship With Your Spouse
Let's Take a Walk Down Memory Lane
Intimacy and Sex, What Do We Need and Want?
Client Story
Could You Please
Connecting to your Spouse's Career but not Wearing the Rank!
The Dreaded D Word...
Deployments
Deployment Exercise
Together but apart...
Here are a few examples to keep the connection alive.
Homecoming!
Client's Deployment Story
Exercise 10
Spouse Connection
Your Family Connection
Find Your Tribe - The Friendship Connection
Exercise 11
Friend Connection
Breaking Up is Always Hard to Do

Chapter 3   129
Ambition

Client story
How Do I Keep Moving Forward with my Career and Education?
Finding the Work you Love
Exercise 12 - Career and Education
Client Testimony

Chapter 4   153
Play!

Exercise 13 - Physical Play
Get Creative!
Exercise 14 - Creative Play
Hobbies Can Help!
Get Goofy!

Chapter 5   167
Inner Peace

Self-Care
Meditation
Exercise 15 - A Basic Meditation
Hot Towel Scrub
Massage & Touch
Mindful Living and
Spirituality
Journaling
Here is my list for today:
Let's Purge!
A Senses Journal
Is there something else you'd like to generate in your journal?
Exercise 16 – Mindful Living Action Steps
On the Road Again…
Exercise 17 - Face Your Fears

Chapter 6   199
Vitality

I'll start on Monday…!
Whole Foods
Exercise 18 - Pantry and Freezer Overhaul
Carbohydrates and Their Bad Rap!
What is a Protein?
Not All Proteins Are Created Equally
Leaner Options
Plants…Yum!
Fats, the Good the Bad and the Ugly!
Saturated Fat
Monounsaturated Fat
Polyunsaturated Fats
Trans Fatty Acid
Exercise 19 - Food Journaling
Getting Organized
Menu Planning
More Tips
Eating Clean During Moving (PCS) Season

Why Do I Get Food Cravings?
Client Story
The Importance of Sleep - Get some Zzz's
Bedtime Tips
Get Active!
What Should I Do, When Should I Do it and Why?
Get a Healthy Heart
Pumping Iron!
Do I Need to Contort Myself into a Pretzel Shape?
Exercise 20 - Vitality Goals
More Tips for Getting It Done, No Excuses!
Home Workout Equipment - What Toys You Need!
What Types of Workouts Should I do?
Functional Resistance   Training Programs
PCS Season Workouts - No Excuses!
Closing

My Hope for You

Testimonies   279

Reviews   283
About The Author

*Don't cry because it's over.
Smile because it happened.
- Dr. Seuss*

Introduction

My Story

Can I share my story with you? Back in 1997, I moved from a small town in Northern England to Hawaii. I had been teaching in a preschool, and I wanted a change, so I took a nannying job. Hawaii was my first experience of America—not a bad start! After being in Hawaii for only six weeks, I fell in love with a military man, a Navy man. Incidentally, this was something we were strongly advised not to do as part of the Au Pair America program. Whoops, I never have been good at following rules!

In the beginning, as with all relationships, we were living an amazing, dreamy and exciting life. Everything was new, fun and an adventure! At the time, my husband at that time was a lieutenant; he had just returned from a deployment onboard a destroyer. He told me of his adventures to places I'd never even dreamed of going. All dressed and dazzlingly handsome in his summer whites, he'd proudly take me on board ship for various events, and I'd meet military spouses, some new, some seasoned. But in all that time, I never considered what my life would be like if I were 'one of them.'

Fast forward 18 months. After another deployment and six months apart, my husband got transferred to Washington DC, which was unexpected, and I followed. We got married! Still, I would say I was disengaged from the military, and looking back I would say even more so disconnected, given we were now on 'shore duty' in a booming metropolis of a city, living in an apartment building. I could not work at that time as I was waiting on acquiring my Green Card and visas. Looking back, it is easy to say I felt isolated and lonely. My husband was stationed in the Pentagon; he had a demanding job and worked long hours. I lived in my bubble of a world, working out at the gym, writing letters home and making a home for us in this new 'America' where I was now living. This America was nothing like the Hawaii America, as you can imagine!

Fast forward ten years, two children and six moves. Although by this point in my life I had been living a military spouse's life, I was at war with myself on a regular basis. I'd meet military spouses who seemed either bitter about their lives or happy with where they were in life. I just did not get it. How can they be so happy when their spouses are always working long hours, commuting for hours on end, deployed, moving all the time or picking up the pieces of children's broken hearts as they said goodbye to their moms or dads once again? This disconnect in my life made me very unhappy, sometimes lonely and often at odds with my husband. I was often on an emotional roller coaster ride of feelings. One month I'd be thankful for my life—after all, I had a great life. I was lucky to have a beautiful home, good health, a family that loved me, and a husband who just wanted me to feel happy. But other times I was filled with the opposite, frustration, resentment and anger. I did not know how to be satisfied with the military life I had.

Sure, I was happy with many other aspects of my life, but it was disconnected from my military spouse life. I could not see the trees in the forest because high rises were blocking my view. How could I change how I felt? After all, people would say to me, "Well you knew what you were getting into when you got married." But do we? I'd imagined married life to be different than my reality. I'm not sure in what way I dreamed it would be different, but I knew it wasn't what I was experiencing. I have always been quite a practical person, so I never dreamt of a fairy tale romance. But I also didn't understand how to be in the role of a military spouse or how to build a life for myself. I felt that every time I was building something, a roadblock came into view and I'd get frustrated. Can you relate to this? Those roadblocks were the typical challenges all military spouses face—moving, finding a new job, new clients, leaving friends behind, seeing my husband leave on a deployment, and being a single parent again. Looking back I now see many ways I could have changed how I perceived my world, but when you are in the middle of emotional turmoil, it is not always easy to rationalize and see a way forward. I'm sure you can relate to this.

Fast forward to 2011, now well over ten moves, living in a sun-filled San Diego home on the base with a husband deployed. This was my first experience of living on a base even though my husband had been in the Navy for over 23 years at this point in our lives. Our children were then in preschool and second grade. Being a temporary single parent to our children was not a new experience. I knew I could do it, living alone. I could confidently raise our children by myself. I'd always been independent; after all, I'd owned my own home in the U.K. when I was only 22 and worked two jobs. I'd left all my family and friends behind and emigrated to a new country—I got this! But the phrase 'I got this' was so ingrained in my mind that I rarely asked for help. I would pioneer on no matter what came my way. I had always been this way, even before I married my sailor. I rarely reached out for help. Being at peace with my military life was still a huge challenge. I did not walk around every day playing the martyr. I had friends, although saying goodbye over and over again saddened my heart. I had a life but huge aspects of it felt amiss.

I had my personal training and Pilates business and clients that I loved, but found it frustrating starting all over again with every move. These were just some of the feelings I was experiencing. There was a constant nagging in the back of my mind, while endless dreams of my husband getting out of the Navy loomed over me like an overcast sky on a winter's day.

Can you relate to this little story of mine?

My Aha Moment

As a goal-oriented person, I decided to take training to become a certified health coach. I certified with the Institute for Integrative Nutrition (IIN). I enrolled in the training with the idea of being able to coach my clients on not only exercise but also nutrition and lifestyle changes. I knew it would add to my already existing business as a Pilates instructor, nutrition specialist, and personal trainer. What I didn't realize was how profoundly it was going to change my life.

We are now in 2012. After a beautiful reunion with my husband's return from an almost 11-month deployment, our family was together once again. But something inside me had changed. Everyone noticed I was morphing myself and creating a new vision for my life. I had essentially health coached myself during my training with IIN. I had a new and positive outlook on my military life. It felt like a summer's day every day! A cloud had lifted and I could see my future. My life now had meaning just like the lyrics by the band Timbuk3, where they sing about a bright future, one so bright they have to wear shades (I'm showing my age—I was 16 when this song hit the charts!).

Peace at Last

I remember the day; it was the fall of 2013. My husband and I were walking our dog around Fort Adams in Newport, Rhode Island, and I said to him, "Looking back I'm not sure I would have chosen this life for myself, but I'm not sure I would not want it either. I'm OK with moving and starting over again."

The look on my husband's face was one of awe, surprise, love, and pride all rolled into one!

It took many years for me to get to the place I'm at today, but I got there, and that is why I decided to write this book. I wanted to share with you that you are not alone; thousands of military spouses feel the same way. Often people don't share their feelings for fear of being judged or being seen as a complainer. It does not matter if you are a new spouse or a seasoned spouse, we all need support and help in finding answers to our unique challenges.

I want to empower you to live a fulfilled, amazing, awesome, sparkling life with cherries on top! Sure, not every day can be an ice cream sundae kind of day, and that's OK! Life will always send a cliffhanger in your path that you will need to figure out how to traverse. How we perceive these challenges and the tools we use to get through them are crucial to your success.

Let me help you become stronger, confident and ready to take on your life.

How to Use this Book

In this book, you will delve into the many different areas of your life and question what it is that you want. Please read the book systematically beginning with chapter one and completing all the exercises. This first chapter and the exercises within it lay the ground work in discovering who you are and what you want. From there, continue to read the subsequent chapters 2-6. Each chapter covers one of the *5 Power Areas* of your life: *Connection, Ambition, Play, Inner Peace And Vitality*. While reading each chapter, you will continue to be drawn back to your original thoughts that you came up with in chapter one. After reading the book you may want to go back and revisit certain chapters again—that's great. I envision you reading this book and using the practical information as you move through different phases of your life as a military spouse. It is going to help you discover how you can grow a fulfilled life with a transient lifestyle.

I can see some of you rolling your eyes about now thinking to yourself, I've read self-help books. I've tried many things in the past, but it did not work, or it's just not worth it...Is the devil of self-doubt sitting on your shoulder muttering little stories that you are all too used to listening to? Let those negative thoughts subside for a moment. Are you ready for change? The life you have right now is precious; this is the real deal. There is no dress rehearsal! I'll ask you once again, are you ready for change? Listen to your gut. What's it telling you about that one simple question I just asked you?

Put your trust in me and join me on an adventure of self-discovery. This will be a journey that will enable you to see the trees in your forest with the sun shining through the leafy canopies. Do you want more from your life? Do you feel you are always waiting for something to change, or to get better or easier? If you answered 'Yes!' then you're in the right place!

By reading this book, you will create a military life for yourself that you will be content and happy with. You will be living in a place where you can make your dreams a reality even when the challenges of being a military spouse come knocking on your door!

Are you ready to have a different vision for your life? When you have finished reading this book and you are putting into practice the ideas you developed along the way, you will have the confidence, the tools, and a passion for following your dreams no matter what curve balls your military life throws at you. I know you can do this. "How?" I hear you ask. Simply because I did it and I've coached many military spouses from different backgrounds with different challenges and helped them to succeed, and now it's your turn. It's that easy. Just say yes to change and you are ready to go. How do you know you are ready for change? Because you bought this book and that was your first step.

Chapter 1

Who Am I?

Let me tell you about my coaching.

I coach predominantly military spouses and active duty military, but I also coach civilian clients. My clients' ages range from late twenties to fifty-five plus. Every session I coach, I see the positive changes my clients are making in their lives. It is an incredible feeling to help people change and no longer feel trapped by their lives. It is inspiring to watch people create, grow and experience a new life they never thought possible.

My work as a health coach covers what *IIN likes to call Primary Food and Secondary Food. The Institute for Integrative Nutrition® (IIN®) founder, Joshua Rosenthal, coined the terms Primary Food and Secondary Food. Primary Food refers to everything that feeds us that is not food. Primary Food such as our careers, relationships, spirituality, physical activity, finances, education, environment, social life, and other lifestyle factors play an equal if not more significant role in the quality of our lives than what is on our plates.

In contrast, Secondary Food is the actual food we eat: fruits, vegetables, grains, proteins, and fats. Secondary Food does not provide the fulfillment Primary Food provides, but oftentimes we use it to suppress our hunger for Primary Food.

Remember, people need more than their nutritional needs met in order to be healthy; they need love, movement, stability, adventure, purpose, and creativity in order to thrive. © Integrative Nutrition Inc. Integrative Nutrition Inc. does not endorse the content contained in this book.

When it comes to what we eat, one diet does not fit all. When I work with clients, I am not 'putting them on a diet; I am creating a sustainable way of eating, a way of fueling your body that you can maintain for the rest of your life without feeling deprived. Let's face it, diets don't work! Fad diets play on your emotions and burn a hole in your wallet as you yet again spend more money trying another new shake, herbal tea, food supplement or appetite suppressant, or a how-to book that vows these are the golden rules to shedding the weight once and for all. We need to make this madness stop!

The other important factor we need to recognize is that we all have bio individual needs. The Institute for Integrative Nutrition® teaches the term "bio-individuality", which is the concept that no one diet or lifestyle works for everyone. Each person's nutritional needs are individual and are based on a number of varying factors such as lifestyle, occupation, climate, age, gender, culture, and religion. Lifestyle needs are individual as well; what works for one person may not work for another with regard to relationships, exercise, career, spirituality, and physical activity. Additionally, people's needs change over time, so it is important to check in with yourself as you evolve.

© Integrative Nutrition Inc. does not endorse the content contained in this book

Take a moment to think about the dynamics of what makes up your life and feeds your soul. It is surely a long list of thoughts. We are complex beings—that's for sure! Together we are going to explore five different areas of your life: *Ambition, Inner Peace, Connection, Play, and Vitality*. From my coaching experience, these seem to be the areas that military spouses tend to need the most guidance in. I am going to call this group your *5 Power Areas*. These five places are where you have the POWER to change your thoughts and lifestyle outcome. The *5 Power Areas* are the places where all of our daily living events happen. It is where our thoughts, feelings, and decisions are made about all the things that affect us in our lives. Within these *5 Power Areas*, we experience happiness, anger, sadness, resentment, joy, elation, peace, pleasure, rage and so on. Finding balance within your *5 Power Areas* is key to your success. The food that satiates your hunger and brings you comfort will balance itself out when you are at one with the other areas of your life. Does this make sense? I often joke with clients that it doesn't matter if I talk to you about eating leafy greens until the cows come home; it won't be helpful if you are struggling with how to transition with your next military move or with a relationship that you can see is being taxed negatively. You cannot have one without the other; you must be in the balance with all the *5 Power Areas*. After that, the rest will become easier.

As you read this book, you will begin to see how all the *5 Power Areas* fuse together with your personal life experiences and how they tie up to your emotions and the all the decisions you make in your life.

We will corroborate the *5 Power Areas* with the *4 Cornerstones of Life*, which are change, flexibility, acceptance, and empathy. We will talk about the *4 Cornerstones of Life* later on.

This simple mind map will serve as a tool for you to generate your ideas and thoughts about what you want your military life to look like.

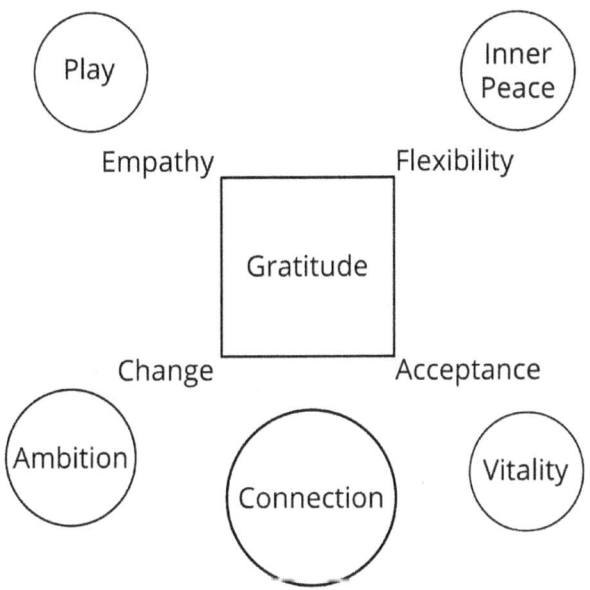

Client Testimony

Here is a statement from a military spouse who completed a three-month coaching program with me. She initially came to me with a weight loss goal, but after our first couple of meetings, she discovered that she was feeling unfulfilled with her life and needed help orientating a new path. She had not worked outside of the home for some time and she missed that. With all the moves and always putting her children first, she was busy. But it did not seem like enough. She felt as though she had lost herself. She had been so consumed with all of her military moves and her spouse's career that she no longer considered what she wanted. She had not realized how much she missed the feeling of workplace success outside of the home. She felt guilty when she craved her old career days. She was preparing for another move and together we got her thinking about what that would look like for her. We strategized and came up with goals and ideas.

When I began with Navenka, I thought I would be learning about nutrition and quite frankly how to eat healthily. Never did I imagine that health coaching would teach me how to look inward and listen to what my body was telling me it needed not just with food but everything else in my life. Navenka showed me how to connect particular food cravings to fatigue, daily activities and everyday stresses of life. Through my short journey, I learned how to listen to my body. Learning how to read my body helped me to understand when & why I would have certain cravings. Navenka taught me how to understand those cravings, which in turn helped me to manage those times when all I wanted to do is binge. Setting small goals in the beginning that may not necessarily be associated with weight loss prepared me mentally to handle the physical challenges at a later date in my coaching. While my intention was simply weight loss when I signed up with Navenka, I received so much more than just nutrition counseling. Having a health coach helped me to look at my living environment and the emotional connection to food. Now I understand that I am eating to heal my body and not eating to comfort myself from the everyday stresses of life.

Your Life Is Happening Now. Is it Making you Happy?

Wait, what, this is my life right now—how can that be? It's not what I planned and I'm not feeling whole. But that's OK because when we move to….It'll be….or when I go on vacation to ….or after deployment I'll…or when my spouse gets out of the service we'll... Does this little conversation sound familiar? It goes right alongside the 'I could have, I would have, I should have devils of doubt' as I like to call them. I could have done… I should have done….you get my point. The quote by Charles Dickens *"Procrastination is the thief of time, collar him,"* rings true here. Have you felt like this? Let's talk about how to change this mindset.

In Richard Carlson's book You Can Be Happy No Matter What, he states, *"Happiness is a state of mind, not a set of circumstances."* [1]

This means that regardless of where you live, you can be happy with the life you have right now. When we look outside of ourselves in search of happiness, we often look at situations and places and sometimes materialistic things. This will not satisfy us but rather leave us with a feeling of unrest. When we live in a bubble of dreaming about how we wish our lives looked and how the future should look, we are robbing ourselves of living in the present. This often leads to dissatisfaction and resentment.

Perhaps you can relate to this situation, for example, you have been saving up for that one particular thing, maybe a down payment on a car, a piece of jewelry or a massage, and now you have enough money to make it happen. This is a small situational happiness event. You feel joy, elation, and excitement, right? Everything in your world seems right again. But after the event passes, you are back to the reality of your world in which you temporarily escaped. You took your attention away from what you think you need but don't have. My point here is that to be happy and content in life we have to create a life that sustains that.

Richard Carlson states, "*You can stop trying to be happy and simply be happy.*" [2]

But how? I hear you ask.

Take Action!

If we are to live this purpose-driven life filled with happiness and gratitude, we must take action. If we do not take action, nothing will change. Have you ever been in a position where you write down your 'to do list' only to find that days or even weeks later you have not been able to check anything off your list? A counselor once told me that if your 'to do list' is empty you are not living a full life! That's an interesting concept as society leads us to believe that to be successful we should get everything checked off the list, right? This, in turn, makes us stressed and worn out always trying to reach the end of the yellow sticky note full of intentions. I believe you should view your to do list as an ongoing reminder of things you would like to accomplish, goals you want to achieve, ambitions you are striving for.

We will discuss ways in which you can check off items on your list by setting goals that are achievable. Having an attainable plan will reduce the anxiety that oftentimes accompanies achieving goals. In his book Intentional Living renowned author and motivational speaker John Maxwell states, *"When I talk about intentional living, I'm describing a life that brings you daily satisfaction and continual rewards."*[3] The message John Maxwell is trying to portray is that there are people in the world who are brimming with fantastic ideas, but they get so overwhelmed with them they do nothing about it. They listen to the devils of doubt too much and fall into a slump of doing nothing and feeling stuck in a rut. We need to take action with our lives! When we are proactive and we set ourselves goals and achieve them, we feel successful. Success brings a feeling of pride, contentment, and happiness. Everybody deserves to feel this way.

How often can you honestly say, hand on your heart, that you feel proud of who you are and what you are accomplishing? When I talk about taking action, it does not have to be a life-changing event; it can be a small step.

How important is it to you to challenge your personal growth? What could you be doing right now that would satisfy you?

I love this quote from John Maxwell:

"When you know what you want and can't find what you need, you must create what you need, so you can get what you want!" [4]

There are a variety of ways to set goals for yourself. One analogy I like is *The Big Rocks Theory* by *Dr. Stephen Covey. He explains a way to prioritize short and long term goals by visualizing a large jar, and in that jar you place some big rocks. Think of those big rocks as your priority goals. For example, it could be researching a continuing education opportunity you may have or revamping your resume. Next, you add some pebbles to the jar; the pebbles represent smaller jobs but things that need to get done to make the big rocks happen.

For example, the steps you would need to take to begin researching the school opportunity. The pebbles you add can also be representative of everyday jobs such as grocery shopping, laundry, time with friends, etc. Last, visualize adding sand and water to the jar; it can hold a lot, right? When we look at our daily routines, we can prioritize our goals, making them achievable. The sand and the water enhance the picture in our minds that we have created; it helps us to understand that we can accomplish quite a lot providing we take action on our goals.

What would happen, do you think, if you put the sand in the jar first? The sand represents all these time-consuming things that distract you from taking action on your goals, for example, social media, emails, phone calls, etc. If you pile the rocks on top of the sand, the jar will not hold as much. You get the message, right?

    Some people prefer to set their goals daily or weekly. Others like to work on monthly goals and even long term, both quarterly and yearly. How you work on your goals is personal to you and your schedule. Below I will show you an example of how you may choose to schedule your action steps to achieve daily and weekly goals. I like to break down my big and small goals into achievable smaller action steps so that they are not overwhelming.

The Scenario

Your spouse has just been given a new duty station. You are on the move again! You had to leave your old job behind working in real estate. You know that the second income is needed for your growing family, and so you plan to work in your new location. You also want to make some new friends and continue practicing yoga.

Step 1 Big Goal - Find work in real estate

Action Steps

Step1 - Research all the real estate offices in your new location that you would be interested in working for.

Step 2 - Update your resume.

Step 3 - Write a cover letter to send with your resume.

Step 4 - Mail out your resumes and letters.

Step 5 - Follow up with a phone call one week later.

Step 6 - Talk with military friends to see who has lived in your new location - do they know anyone in real estate?

Date and Time - attach a date and time you will work on your action steps and write them on your calendar.

Step 1 - 17th June 9-11AM
Step 2 - 18th June 1-3 PM
Step 3 - 19th June 2-4 PM
Step 4 - 20 June 9-11 AM
Step 5 - 21st June 5-6 PM
Step 6 – 22nd June 1-2 PM

Step 2 Smaller Goal - Finding a yoga studio

Action Steps

Step 1- Research the yoga studios online.

Step 2 - Narrow it down to 2-3 choices and visit them.

Step 3 - Make a date to try the complimentary class they have on offer and mark it on your calendar.

Step 4 - Attend the class, sign up for a membership, and make some new friends.

Using this idea will allow you to plan and execute your daily, weekly and monthly goals. Pencil in the steps in your calendar and stick to the project just like you would any other appointment. You wouldn't just not show up to a doctor or dentist appointment or a planned lunch with a friend, would you? Treat this with just as much respect—turn up, do the work and see the results unfold. It's a simple but effective process. Use this basic template or alternately take a look online; there are many printable templates for goal setting and tons of ideas on Pinterest too.

Bucket List Goals

I am associating your bucket list goals with the bigger life goals that you may have. For example, you may want to go back to school to study a degree in fine arts or perhaps you want to take a vacation to a Hawaiian island. You can use the action steps I described above to set time in your schedule to make the bigger life events come to fruition. Break down your action steps and assign a time to each step along with a date you wish to achieve it by.

In our fast-paced lives, there are also the mundane tasks that we need to get done like grocery shopping, scheduling appointments, and cleaning the house. Be sure when you plan your weekly schedule that you are making time for all these items to be checked off your list. Set days and times that you will give to each job. Don't turn up late for chore duty and don't allow yourself to run over. Clock in and clock out! Remember your big goals and bucket list items are your priority.

To ensure we keep a balanced life, we must allow ourselves time to play. We will talk much more about this later on. But when you are busy fulfilling your steps and action plans, don't forget your friends and family. You need downtime; we all need to rest, relax and have fun. Put it on your calendar just like you would any other important event.

What Do I Want?
The Million Dollar Question!

Now that's a loaded question with quite possibly a mountain of thoughts and ideas attached to it. When I begin coaching a client, I like to ask them this question. It is interesting observing their body language and hearing their thoughts. I'd say more often than not my clients have a difficult time coming up with an answer. They just don't know where to begin. For some it has been so long since someone asked them this question that they get quite upset and bubbling out of them comes a string of emotions ranging from guilt, fear, and self-doubt.

Often, people dare not to dream because they put all their ideas in a perfect box, neatly tied with a bow on top. I wish life could be that way, but that is not the reality of anyone's life whether they are a military spouse or not. This way of thinking is too rigid. People who expect things to be a certain way often give up when they cannot achieve it. Don't let that person be you. When we limit our existence to circumstance, we limit the endless possibilities this amazing life has to offer.

As a military spouse, you have to be flexible! I know some of you are already good at this. All it takes is practice, just like anything else in our lives. In exercising flexibility, you will create a habit that will serve you well as your military life unfolds. I understand how often you find yourself making compromises for all kinds of things in your daily life simply because it is a little easier that way. Making compromises is a useful life skill. However not to the point that we lose ourselves and forget about our personal needs and wants. When we examine what we want our lives to look like today, we first have to take into consideration that we cannot compare our lives to that of spouses in the civilian world.

We have to get more creative in continuing to strive for what we want for this life to work for us. That being said, I am not telling you that you will never get what your heart desires. I am just stating the obvious fact that we have a transient life, so we must flex our imaginations more so and allow our tree branches to blow with the wind. That way we can experience a more positive outcome. As a military spouse, you have many amazing gifts that other people in the civilian world are not as well equipped with. I'm talking here about the *4 Cornerstones: Change, Flexibility, Empathy*, and proudly standing tall next to those chaps is *Acceptance*! The last one is still a work in progress for me!

I went through a period where I would say the words out loud to help me take it on board and believe in it! It didn't matter if I was in line at the post office, grocery shopping in the commissary or at home alone; if an appointment I had was running very late, I'd say to myself 'acceptance!'. If our orders changed as they so often do…acceptance. If my husband could not spend time with us on the weekend due to work commitments, again I'd shout out 'acceptance!' If the kids were arguing over whose turn it was to take out the garbage, you got it…acceptance! It's surprising how this simple word helped me to be calmer and more level headed in dealing with many situations. Try it, but watch out for those around you—when you belt out those words of wisdom, you may get some funny looks! Remember you have to believe in the words for them to take effect. If you begin practicing acceptance in your daily life, you will have more peace.

When you turn acceptance around and look at what is on the opposite end of it, you may experience empathy, this being the last of the *4 Cornerstones of Life*. Empathy for the person who is also inconvenienced and more often than not finds themselves in a situation which is beyond their control. Of course, your spouse would love to spend quality time with you on the weekends, but if his/her boss has pressing work to do, that is where your spouse has to be. Naturally, the doctor does not want to run late for her appointments that day, sending all her patients into a tailspin and running the risk of giving them high blood pressure, or likewise your spouse's orders are sometimes out of control of the person we believed had it all in control. Imagine their frustration, not just your own. Showing empathy, practicing acceptance, having flexibility and dealing with change is no easy task.

When we think about these *4 Cornerstones Of Life—Flexibility, Change, Acceptance, And Empathy*—we have to work on them all with an air of gratitude. Gratitude just means we feel thankful. It could mean being thankful for what someone has done for us or merely for our everyday existence. It is interesting to think that gratitude rhymes with attitude! I live by the words 'what we think about comes about'. *Gratitude* is like the glue bonding everything together. Was Rome built in a day? No! Be kind and patient with yourself as you navigate these four cornerstones and practice bringing gratitude into your life. As you work through this book, you will gain a solid foundation of how to do just that, making the *4 Cornerstones of Life* gel together.

Listen to Your Gut; It Will Tell You What You Want

    I remember back when I was studying to become a health coach I decided to begin practicing meditation. Some meditations were silent meditations and others were guided meditations. My focus was on self-discovery meditations. Through my practice, I learned how to listen to my gut. You've heard of the saying 'Trust your gut instinct.' I think that it is more than just a phrase. I believe that the gut is where the truth sits in all of us.

    When you ask yourself the question "What do I want?" your gut may give you a straightforward answer. For example, it may be telling you to take the job offer at the realtor's office or take the volunteer position at your son's school. Or there may be more subtle words filling your mind. When I did this exercise for the first time, the word PEACE just came to me over and over again. I remember tears streaming down my face as that same word filled the room like a massive vortex waiting to suck me in. At the time, I felt confused. Why was I crying? What did I want peace with? How would I get it? You may experience something similar. Don't worry, we will work on whatever it is you are hearing and help you get the clarity you need.

Exercise 1 - What Do I Want?

Take a moment—sit quietly by yourself, placing one hand on your heart's center and one hand on your belly, and take a deep inhalation through your nose and exhale slowly through your mouth. Do this five times. With each breath, feel the rise and fall of your belly and chest. Make a connection with the simple act of finding peace and quiet with the breath. This simple breathing technique will help to quieten your monkey mind and all its constant running thoughts. You should begin to feel more centered.

Now ask yourself, "What do I want?" Listen to what your gut is telling you.

Ask again, "What do I want?"

Listen and ask again.

You can repeat this as many times as you wish. Some clients have told me they have sat there for 5 minutes, others 25 minutes or more. The first time I tried this exercise, I sat there asking and listening until I felt spent, until I could hear nothing. When you do this exercise, your only goal is to observe the breath and listen to the thoughts that arise. I don't expect you to find answers to what you hear your gut telling you. I also don't want you to hold any attachments to what you hear. Have patience, listen and ask, observe how you feel.

    My clients have shared with me that after doing this simple exercise, they realize that they have been neglecting themselves. They hear what their gut is telling them and they begin to understand that they have not been allowing themselves to live their dreams. Sometimes that leads to a feeling of anxiety and sadness.

Client Story

I had a client tell me that the words "own a home" kept coming to her when she did this exercise. When we looked deeper into what that could mean for her, we discovered that she didn't want to buy and own a home of her own; she wanted to feel secure with each move and be at peace with wherever she called home. She also wanted to feel at home in her own body. I find this to be a focus area for most of my clients. At home in your own body can mean different things for each of us. For this particular client, it meant accepting her body with the few extra pounds she was carrying and loving herself for who she was as well as thriving and not just surviving the military moves. We will talk more about this later.

Client Story

Another client wanted to take vacations all the time; her gut was pumping out beaches, lake houses and all kinds of dreamy, exotic travel plans! It was true it had been a long period since her family had taken a vacation. But when we took a deeper look into her thoughts, we connected them to the need for more excitement in her life, balanced with more peace. She was bored with the same routine and did not know how to break out of old habits. A holiday to a lake house was just the thing to ease her mind and soul. But naturally she could not always be taking trips away, as alluring as that seemed! Together we worked on how we could change her boredom and get her to feel excited about her daily life.

We also worked on how to find solitude in her day. If you can connect to these two clients' experiences, you are not alone. This is not a unique situation, far from it. I will give you the tools you need as you progress through this book to get you the life you want whatever that means to you.

Exercise 2 - Making Your Gut Instinct List

In the next step, please write down all the words that came up when you asked your gut what you wanted. Make a list, but in doing so do not try to answer the questions. Don't cross anything off your list thinking it is silly or irrelevant. Nothing that our mind creates is irrelevant; there is a reason for most things. Go ahead, spend some time now making your list of what you want.

Your list is unique to you. But for clarity in understanding, in this exercise your list may have words/phrases such as:

- better health
- weight loss
- patience
- fun
- work/job
- exercise plan
- intimacy
- romance
- organization
- quiet time
- relaxation
- a new car
- a new home
- happiness

- less anxiety
- a good relationship with my mom
- a better relationship with my daughter

Exercise 3 - Build Your Mind Map

I'd like you to make some mind maps. You may have made something like this when you were in language arts class when you were planning out ideas for a story you were going to write. You're now going to build your life story using these mind maps.

Write each of the following *5 Power Area* words on a blank piece of paper or in a journal:

- Connection
- Ambition
- Inner Peace
- Vitality
- Play

Draw a bubble around each word.

In the following chapters, we will explore each of these *5 Power Areas.* You have the POWER to set goals within these areas and create a life you love.

Below is a piece written by Danaan Parry called "The Parable of The Trapeze." It is taken from his book Warriors of the Heart.[5]

As you read, take note of what the words are saying and how they relate to your life. How do you feel after reading this piece?

Sometimes I feel that my life is a series of trapeze swings. I'm either hanging on to a trapeze bar swinging along or, for a few moments in my life; I'm hurtling across space in between trapeze bars.

Most of the time, I spend my life hanging on for dear life to my trapeze-bar-of-the-moment. It carries me along at a certain steady rate of swing and I have the feeling that I'm in control of my life.

I know most of the right questions and even some of the answers.

But every once in a while as I'm merrily (or even not-so-merrily) swinging along, I look out ahead of me into the distance and what do I see? I see another trapeze bar swinging toward me. It's empty and I know, in that place in me that knows, that this new trapeze bar has my name on it. It is my next step, my growth, my aliveness coming to get me. In my heart of hearts I know that, for me to grow, I must release my grip on this present, well-known bar and move to the new one.

Each time it happens to me I hope (no, I pray) that I won't have to let go of my old bar completely before I grab the new one. But in my knowing place, I know that I must totally release my grasp on my old bar and, for some moment in time, I must hurtle across space before I can grab onto the new bar.

Each time, I am filled with terror. It doesn't matter that in all my previous hurtles across the void of unknowing I have always made it. I am each time afraid that I will miss, that I will be crushed on unseen rocks in the bottomless chasm between bars. I do it anyway. Perhaps this is the essence of what the mystics call the faith experience. No guarantees, no net, no insurance policy, but you do it anyway because somehow to keep hanging on to that old bar is no longer on the list of alternatives. So, for an eternity that can last a microsecond or a thousand lifetimes, I soar across the dark void of "the past is gone, the future is not yet here." It's called "transition." I have come to believe that this transition is the only place where real change occurs. I mean real change, not the pseudo-change that only lasts until the next time my old buttons get punched.

I have noticed that, in our culture, this transition zone is looked upon as a "no-thing," a no-place between places. Sure, the old trapeze bar was real, and that new one coming towards me, I hope that's real, too. But the void in-between? Is that just a scary, confusing, disorientating nowhere that must be gotten through as fast and as unconsciously as possible?

NO! What a wasted opportunity that would be. I have a sneaking suspicion that the transition zone is the only real thing and the bars are illusions we dream up to avoid the void where the real change, the real growth, occurs for us. Whether or not my hunch is true, it remains that the transition zones in our lives are incredibly rich places. They should be honored, even savored. Yes, with all the pain and fear and feelings of being out of control that can (but not necessarily) accompany transitions, they are still the most alive, most growth-filled, passionate, expansive moments in our lives.

References:

You Can Be Happy No Matter What 5 principles for keeping life in perspective 15th Edition 2007   1,2113,131

The 7 Habits of Highly Effective People - Stephen R Covey

Intentional Living Choosing a Life That Matters 2015 - John Maxwell 3, 4 29, 37

Warriors Of The Heart The Trapeze Parable Danaan Parry 1991 5 84-85,   Used by permission.

*Steven Covey Web 2017
https://www.youtube.com/watch?v=ZHne8c5qg0g

Chapter 2

Connection

When you think of the word connection, what picture do you create in your mind? What or whom are you connecting with? From the moment we are conceived and life is creating in our mother's body, we experience our very first connection. In the womb, we are hearing sounds of our mother's body, her voice, her digestion, her heartbeat. The miracle of birth takes place, and from that moment on we begin to form relationships and bonds with everyone who touches our lives in both positive and negative ways. This journey continues to be built upon layer by layer. This pilgrimage of life, if you like, continues until the day we die. It's incredible to think about the thousands of connections you will have in your lifetime. Let's separate and explore these connections into groups.

Your Relationship with Yourself...

How do you view your relationship with yourself? Do you like yourself, or are you disappointed with yourself? Do you value yourself or do you feel you are not worthy? Are you bored with yourself or do you see yourself as someone always on the go with no time to slow down? We first need to identify how we see ourselves. The reason for this is so we can create a stable relationship with number 1! Me, myself and I!

The most important relationship we can have is the one with ourselves. When we have positive feelings about ourselves, we grow into secure people. We have to love ourselves first so that we can love others and give more freely. When we truly understand who we are and we understand our needs and wants, then we can be a better and happier wife, husband, parent, friend, colleague, sister, brother and so on. For some of you, this way of thinking may sound selfish or too proud. But let's face it, if we don't hold ourselves in high regard and if we only consider ourselves middling to fair, how will we be perceived by others? What you think about comes about, right? You will hear me say this over and over again because it's true. The very thought of holding yourself in high esteem may be making you very uncomfortable right about now.

Just reading the words in print may make you feel too self-centered. But why?

All the thoughts and feelings you have today have been created from experiences you have had in your life, as both an adult and a child, both negative and positive. Some of you may have had a connection within a past relationship that made you feel insecure with who you are. Maybe during that time in your life that particular relationship, either personal or professional, destroyed all the things that make up who you identified yourself as. Or perhaps as a child you were raised in a conservative home environment and taught that modesty was the right way to behave. Maybe you were never given the opportunity to explore the relationship you have with yourself. It could be that your parents never expressed their feelings toward you or loved you up as much as they could have. If you are a parent, how often do you ask your child to describe to you who they are and what positive traits they have? Have you ever asked your child to describe what kind of a person they see themselves as and how they want to be perceived? Try it and see what comes up for your son or daughter or even your spouse. Ask them to make a verbal list of traits that describe how they see themselves.

Your opinions of yourself also come from the daily internal conversations that you have. When I am coaching clients, I find that these one-sided conversations torment and demoralize a person's spirit and leave them feeling lost. I call them the good angel and the bad angel, one on each shoulder, each one demanding your attention, making judgments, arguments, decisions about you and your feelings, thoughts and ideas. Your mind is a great creator. I'll say that again; *your mind is a great creator.* It creates stories all day long. What kind of story is your brain creating for you, about who you are and where in life you are heading?

Building a solid relationship with yourself does not happen overnight. I am a very different person to the shy teenager I was in high school. Or the young and fiercely independent woman I was in my 20's and 30's. Even now in my late 40's I am still consciously aware of the more subtle changes I make in my outlook on life and my thoughts and feelings about who I am and where I am going. We morph into a variety of different versions of ourselves as we age and grow with life experiences. What we need to work on is the opportunity for you to develop a kind and gentle relationship that you can experience with yourself. I need you to hold close to your heart the great traits of what makes you the amazing person you are.

When you can draw upon this deep sense of self-worth, you will be stronger. When you understand and value the relationship you have with yourself, you are better equipped for situations your life presents. You can identify yourself and trust your individuality; you will be better prepared to ride the waves of your military life with greater ease. When storms come your way, you will be able to draw upon your strength and not allow your boat to be rocked so much that you feel like a shipwreck washed up on the shore. This involves listening to your gut.

As a child, my nana's words were, "Love yourself the most and give others a little of what is left!!" I'm not sure whether this is a perfect scenario or a perfect storm waiting to happen! But you can see where she was coming from! I never thought much about those words growing up, but looking back and remembering the independent, fiery, happy-go-lucky woman my nana was, it is obvious she lived and believed in her self-worth. When she walked into a room, she had a presence about her. She was a petite woman, only 5ft 2", but people always described her as a tall lady! She had confidence, poise, and grace.

Learning the skill of confidence and portraying that to the world is useful as we are often called to use it even if deep down we are feeling insignificant and insecure. I'm not saying you have to fake it till you make it. I want you to BELIEVE in who you are. When you walk into a room of strangers, what do you want people to say about you? Would you agree with them? You may well be asking yourself,

"How do I know who I am?" The following exercises should help you to identify not only who you are but also your personality type and interests.

Exercise 4 - Let's Love Ourselves Up!

Write down all the words that you can think of that describe what you like about yourself. They can be attributes and personality traits. Your list may look like this:

- funny
- kind heart
- energetic
- fun
- patient
- good at sports
- great hair
- awesome legs
- good friend
- hard worker
- fair
- happy-go-lucky

How many things did you write on your list? Was this a challenge for you? Why was it difficult? You may have only been able to come up with a handful of words.

I bet if you asked a child to do this same exercise they would have a much easier time with it. Probably because as parents we build our children up. If we are a good parent, we help to develop our children's confidence. We are always praising our kids, not just for the big things but also for small daily accomplishments. But how often do we praise ourselves? We are good at talking negatively and berating ourselves to the point that it is destructive to our health. But rarely do we love ourselves up.

    Take a moment to think about how often in the day you belittle or verbally beat yourself up over something insignificant. Now imagine you spoke that way to your friends. How many friends do you think you would have if you kept this up? Let's get you talking to yourself like you would to a dear and close friend. That means you have to speak with respect, empathy and patience, right?

Exercise 5 - What You Like About Me

For the next month have your spouse write on a Post-it note a word or phrase of something they like about you. Ask them to stick the note to the bathroom mirror or fridge. Don't be shy to ask; after all, if we don't ask for what we want, we won't get what we need. If they are deployed, ask them to send it in an email even if it's just a one liner or just on the subject line. We know deployments are super busy and we cannot always receive a long love letter! You can also do the same for them if you wish. The goal of this exercise is to read what they wrote and agree with them, no ifs or buts. Just accept it, be thankful, and give gratitude. Take that word with you for the rest of the day and hold it close to your heart. If something upsets you, you can draw on your positivity word bank to pull you back to center and shake off any negativity you may be experiencing. Just like building a house, we have to begin with the foundations. Think of each word as a foundation for building you into a stronger, more resilient person. This takes practice, patience, and of course believing.

Who Am I?

> *The Caterpillar and Alice looked at each other for some time in silence: at last, the Caterpillar took the hookah out of its mouth, and addressed her in a languid, sleepy voice.*
> *'Who are you?' said the Caterpillar.*
> *This was not an encouraging opening for a conversation. Alice replied, rather shyly, 'I—I hardly know, sir, just at present—at least I know who I WAS when I got up this morning, but I think I must have been changed several times since then.'*
>
> *Lewis Carroll, Through the Looking-Glass

I love this quote and I think it is relatable to a military spouse's life! So often we are required to reinvent ourselves with each move we make, taking on a new career or even a new role such as being the stay-at-home parent or a temporary single parent during times of travel and deployment.

Part of exploring the relationship you have with yourself is discovering who you are and what you want.

Exercise 6 - Who Am I?

It is not unusual to have no idea who you are. You may feel that you have lost yourself. You may realize that you have followed your spouse's career for so long that you no longer consider yourself, your desires and needs. Do you feel as though you have put your life on the back burner? Have you been telling yourself this is not your time? Let's change those thoughts.

Take a few minutes to write a list of words describing who you are. Don't think about it, just write

What kinds of things came up for you?

Maybe you are a mother, father, husband; you are a military spouse, a teacher, a chef, a realtor or perhaps a volunteer, a parent, a caretaker. The list is unique to you. What is one thing you notice about this list that unites it together? Did you notice you listed all the jobs you had? When I asked you who you are, I'm guessing most of you described the many hats you wear day to day, right? That's ok, this is who you are. But let's put a different spin on it now.

Exercise 7 - A Deeper Internal Look

Please write a list of words/phrases that describe who you are on a deeper, more personal level. Don't describe the jobs you have; think about your intimate relationships with your spouse, family and friends and your personality traits. Dig deep into your soul and see what words come up.

This time your list may look more like this:

lover, friend, soul mate, sexual, nonsexual, a pleaser, a quitter, a peace seeker, a thrill seeker, head strong, fantasizer, high anxiety, an organizer, an adventurer, agreeable, argumentative, friendly, stubborn, relaxed, fearless, afraid

Exercise 8 - Playful Me!

Lastly, please write a list of words/phrases that describe the playful you, your interests, hobbies, and desires. This list should include things you are interested in trying for the first time. This is your chance to let your mind run wild. Free it from constricting thoughts—think larger than life! Do you need some type of adventure, do you want to achieve a life dream? This should be a fun exercise that brings you joy. It may look like this:

a ceramist, a quilter, a golfer, a poet, a blogger, a writer, a runner, a cyclist, a movie buff, a skier, a rollerblader, a crafter, reader, I want to be a painter, I'd like to try rollerblading, I want to take a trip to the Great Wall of China, I want to see the Pyramids in Egypt, I want to take a French cooking course...

It is surprising what comes out of these exercises, isn't it? You should feel liberated by the power of discovering who you are. I'll bet you are pleasantly surprised by all the different roles you have and all the wonderful ideas and intentions that you have for your life. All of these things make you an incredibly special and unique person. "How do I make them my reality?" I hear you ask. Hang tight, here's how!

Exercise 9 - Mind Map Connections

The next step you need to take is to use your 5 Power Area mind maps that you created earlier and attach the words/phrases you came up with in exercises 1-8. For example, one of the *5 Power Areas* we have listed is

Play. Some of the words in exercise 8 are relatable to this 5 Power Area.

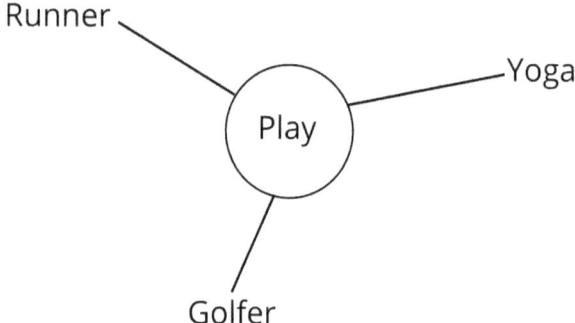

Another example below is Connection. You see some words/phrases you may write.

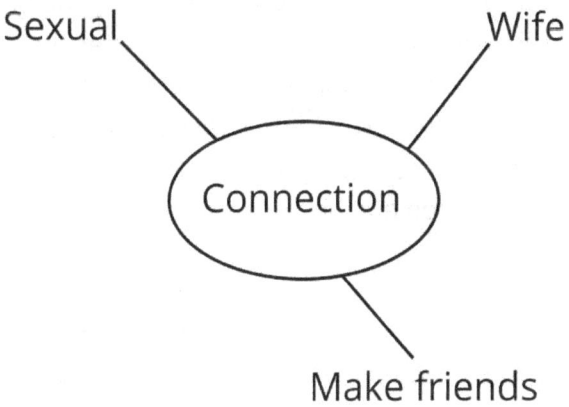

You will notice that some of the words/phrases you listed will repeat in more than one of the *5 Power Areas*. That's fine. As you write you may add more words, ideas and thoughts about what you want your life to look like. Don't hold back. I don't want you to think small; I want you to write down every dream, hope, and desire in each of the *5 Power Areas*. Even if you think it is not attainable, I want you to write it down. For example, under Ambition you may have written, "I'd like my own online Etsy store." Or under Connection you may have written, "I need to find a running buddy." Or you may have expressed a desire to have a date night or to ask your neighbor out for lunch.

Under *Inner Peace*, you may have phases such as begin meditating, try tai chi, and go to yoga class. As another example, maybe under Vitality it may say start drinking green juice, make a home cooked meal, or join boot camp. This exercise will take some time to complete. Don't rush through this; enjoy the process. You may want to keep revising the exercise over the next week. You can add more words and phrases as things come to you.

When you have completed this task, you will have created a better understanding of the relationship you have with yourself and a vision of who you are and what you want. You will visualize the ideas of what your life can and will look like if you step out of your comfort zone and keep moving forward building the life that you deserve. Are you ready for the best roller coaster ride of your life, the kind that fills you with fun even though at times it feels scary?

Building your Independence Muscle!

What does independence look like to you? The first place to develop independence is by accepting yourself. You cannot be independent if you cannot be at peace with yourself. If you are always second guessing your choices with things that are happening in your life, you will always depend on someone to help you make decisions. Always depending on others is not a safe place to be because one day those people you depend on may no longer be there. People move on, and we lose touch, people pass away.

If you build your relationship with yourself, you will never be let down. Have faith in who you are. Begin by first accepting that you have your own thoughts, preferences, and opinions. You will make your own choices and mistakes, and that's OK. You are not in competition with anyone else. Be yourself. Work on being self-motivated. Don't worry if you find that you do not fit in the expected "box." If you want to try a new activity but you don't know anyone else who wants to join you, don't procrastinate—just do it! If you have a desire to follow a particular career path, lose weight, write a book or something else, do these things for yourself because you have the desire to succeed. Don't do it to try to impress others. That is not a place that will make you happy. Your world beliefs should not be swayed by others with the fear of them judging you. Independent thinkers see the world for both the good and the bad. But they stay true to their beliefs so that they can be strong for themselves and others.

If you always have the thought "Oh what will she/he think if I...?" you will never grab opportunities that present themselves to you for fear of being judged by others. Let go of this, don't care what others think, build trust within, and be your fabulous self, flaws and all.

Pressing the Pause Button on Life

Many people out there depend on their partner to bolster their confidence when trying out new experiences or to make new friends. When we depend on our spouses too much and live in that comfort zone, I find that people get lost, especially when their spouse is working long hours or when they are on travel or deployed. When I am coaching military spouses, I work with them on how to build a life of their own. I cannot put enough emphasis on how important this is. Many military spouses I coach are sometimes playing the waiting game. They will put their life on hold. They don't pursue new experiences where they are currently living until their partner can do it with them. Even though this is a kind gesture, it is not an ideal situation to put yourself in. I am all too familiar with this territory; I used to be like this. I'd wait to see that movie or visit that museum or restaurant or I'd wait to take the kids to that particular park until Dad could join us and so on. When you put a pause on your life for too long, you are missing out on wonderful experiences, and before you know it, you'll be moving onto the next duty station. Then you'll be visited by the wish and why twins 'I wish I had…' and 'why did I not do…' in the place of regret. We cannot expect to get all of these new experiences in on the weekends or whenever your spouse is off work. You need to begin building your own life. Being a self-motivator and feeling self-assured will serve you well in your military life.

Don't wait; this is your life right now! You deserve the best life ever, right? Discovering all the possibilities available to you will enrich your life and help you to become more confident and able to flex your independence muscle.

Naturally, with every move we all press stop on our lives. Then there is a pause phase, and eventually we push the play button. We don't get to rewind (I'm using the analogy of a cassette tape player here—I'm showing my age!). Don't wait too long in the pause phase. Start living today! To guide you down this path and into this independent way of thinking, take a moment to imagine you had to leave your current duty station tomorrow. What do you wish you had done? Why have you not done it? Look at your mind maps and see where your interests lie. Look at your calendar and schedule a trip out with yourself and your friends. For some of you, this may be quite scary. It doesn't matter if you are a young spouse or a seasoned spouse, being independent and confident may not be the way you were raised. It may be a territory you have little experience traversing.

    Some people are introverts, others extroverts, but we all have our challenges. I want you to push past your fears and take a leap of faith in yourself. Begin by taking baby steps to building your independence. If you are afraid of going to a restaurant for dinner alone, start with lunchtime and take a good book to read. Or seek out that new volunteer opportunity or connect with that one other spouse who works where you'd like to be hired. If reaching out to a new friend to do something fun seems awkward, go with your gut and do it anyway. Chances are they feel just like you do: lonely, awkward, bored, etc. Eventually, who knows, you may take a vacation with your kids or with a friend or even alone. Step out of your comfort zone. I know you can do this—all you have to do is believe in yourself.

"Man cannot discover new oceans unless he has the courage to lose sight of the shore."

-Andre Gide

The only thing that can come out of pushing yourself is a sense of pride and saying to yourself, "I can do this alone. I got this." Perhaps a new friendship will develop. You will build a better understanding of who you are and how you can enjoy your life even when spending some of it alone. As a military spouse, you know what being alone feels like. But being lonely and being alone are different from each other. Being happy and alone is your goal. Getting comfortable and learning to enjoy your own company is essential. When you decide who you are and what you want, being independent will become easier. You may even enjoy it!

Financial Independence

Having joint bank accounts and the attitude of what's mine is yours and yours is mine is an excellent and positive way of thinking. Sharing everything in a marriage is important. However, some people miss being financially independent. For many military spouses, this is important. If this describes you, find work that appeals to you. The chapter on Ambition will help you with your job search goals. Earning a salary enables you to save your own money, write checks and pay your bills. If you are a stay-at-home parent or unable to work, discuss with your partner about setting some money aside from their paycheck for you to use as you wish. This may give you some more financial freedom. You could also take over the family finances. Perhaps you have always wanted to learn about stocks and shares and you work on growing your family's income that way. Come up with a plan that works for you and your spouse.

Client Story

When I first sought out Navenka's help, I was working in a paint store, a job I did not love, and I felt very stressed and bored. I had a degree in interior design, and I was not using it at my current workplace. I'd lost the confidence to seek what I wanted for my life. There seemed to be too many obstacles in my way. My time with Navenka as my health coach was for getting my life back on track, both mentally and physically, and to lose weight. Navenka was able to guide me into a cleaner lifestyle, including food and overall life choices, during our six months together. She helped me mentally with negative thoughts, stress, and other triggers that are unhealthy. I quit my job and got hired overseeing a design project on a new home build!

We also found out that I am gluten sensitive. With her suggestions I am now avoiding gluten and replacing it with healthy alternatives. I have gained confidence, become stronger, healthier and lost inches around my waist.

What I appreciated most about working with Navenka was her desire to want to work with me. She never made me feel like I was a burden or asking too many questions. She made me feel like we had been good friends for years, not an acquaintance.

Does this story look similar to your life? Sometimes when we are faced with too many obstacles that we cannot figure out how to get around, we feel overwhelmed, and we just give up. If you always give up on what you want from your life, you will get more of the same. Doing the same thing over and over and expecting life to change is not the way forward. You need a system in place and goals that will propel you to live the life you dream of. I can help you get there, but you must trust yourself and believe that you can change.

Your Relationship With Your Spouse

The relationship you have with your spouse is the second most important connection you have, the first, as we discussed earlier, being the relationship with yourself. Although your spouse loves you and wants you to be happy and feel fulfilled with your life, they cannot take ultimate responsibility to get you there. The only person who can make you feel content and fulfilled in this transient lifestyle is you.

When I was collecting research in preparation for writing this book, I sent out some surveys, and one of the concerns that came up from those results was the fact that many of you feel your relationship with your spouse is challenged significantly due to the circumstances of your military lifestyle. This is not shocking news! As a military spouse, you experience many hardships that civilian spouses do not have to consider, such as deployments when your better half is gone for months at a time and unaccompanied tours where they leave for a year or more. Or partners going into war zones and then there is a constant worry for their safety. Those things are compiled with being a temporary single parent and your spouse being away from your children.

Then there are the challenges of reuniting and reconnecting after many separations; it can all take its toll. The question then becomes: How can I keep doing this over and over again? The stress this places on a marriage is enormous. I think we often underestimate how problematic the challenges we face truly are. Most of us just pull up our boot straps and hope for the best, often pushing the anxiety over many of these situations to the back of our minds. We soldier on. However, when we do not address our concerns and reconnect with our partner regularly, things can start to go awry. Eventually, these thoughts and feelings turn into relationship turmoil, until one day you find that you are just going through the motions of day-to-day life and that you have been ignoring the reality of what is happening in your marriage. If you recognize yourself and your spouse to be in a similar situation to this, please seek professional counseling. Your relationship is worth the time and effort, right?

I have heard clients talk about craving consistency, connection, security, support, and simplicity when they describe what they would like their relationship with their spouse to look like. When I ask clients to describe how they would like their relationship to feel, the answers vary from fun, exciting, romantic, and relaxed to stress-free.

We all want to feel loved, heard, supported and connected to our spouses. But just like anything else in our life that eventually becomes a habit, we have to create an environment that supports this. We have to work on our relationship with our spouse just like the one we create for ourselves. We live in a fast and ever-changing world, and what I so often observe within my coaching practice is my clients losing touch with what drew them to their spouse in the beginning. They are swallowed up with the tasks of everyday living. We have work, separations, kids, homes to take care of, possibly aging parents or sick relatives, moves, deployments—we have a LIFE! This is just the reality of the world we live in, and we cannot escape it.

So how can we keep building our foundations with our spouse, how can we grow strong and not estranged? How can we bring back the spark and the romance? How can we work on our intimacy and our sexual relationship?

Let's Take a Walk Down Memory Lane

How did you meet your spouse, where were you, which state or country were you living in? What were you doing when you met? What attracted you to him/her? Was it love at first sight followed by a steamy, hot romance or was it a gradual friendship that turned into a marriage? Did you know from that first meeting that she/he was your soul mate or was there a time of learning who the other person was and deciding if this was a good fit? Perhaps you married early in life or maybe later. Whatever attractions drew you to your spouse should never be forgotten. It is usually a heartwarming tale to tell, the story of how you met and fell in love. The other reason to reminisce back to this time in your life is it brings a wonderful sense of happiness and warmth into your body and along with that come the endorphins of love, connection, and attraction.

    Let's consider some simple tips that I hope will bring you and your spouse closer.

Intimacy and Sex, What Do We Need and Want?

If you are newly married, the area of intimacy may hold no issues for you and your spouse. You are still in a phase of finding out who this person is that you married. But for others who have been married for some time now and have children in the home or even those who are empty nesters, you may find that making time to be intimate may be the last thing on your minds. But it shouldn't be that way.

Client Story

The mother of four young children shared this with me

"I just don't have the energy for intimacy of any kind with my husband after nursing a baby and wiping poopy butts all day and chasing after kids; I've got nothing left to give."

We discovered that even though this was true, she was also having a hard time switching off from one role to another, from being the mom to being the sexy wife her husband missed. But more importantly, she had forgotten all about herself and her needs and goals and desires; it had been buried deep down. She had forgotten one of the *5 Power Areas*, *Connection*, and how that looked with herself and how it looked in their marriage. She had lost her sexy pizazz because she never gave herself time to give some much-needed attention to herself. She rarely prioritized herself. You may be able to relate to this client's story; it is not unique. The stay-at-home parent tends to be the giver, giving of their selves unselfishly day in and day out. We give so much we forget who we are. We find ourselves so lost in a sea of day-to-day business that we no longer work on our dreams and goals and relationships. We will talk more about building your life later in this book. So what can you do to create the intimacy back into your marriage?

It is so important to keep the intimate side of your relationship alive. Intimacy is about connection, play and vitality, within the *5 Power Areas*. When I talk about intimacy with my clients and I ask them how this is going for them, they often talk about sex. Of course sex is a healthy part of your relationship. But don't confuse intimacy with sex. A sexual relationship is intimate, but there are many other ways to express the bond of intimacy that binds you to your spouse. Intimacy is a deeper understanding that the two of you share. It is about being wholly respected, trusted and supported without fear of rejection, criticism or sarcasm. It's about touch, love, friendship, and care.

Your sexual relationship should also channel your deepest feelings for each other. It should be a time of love, fun and some excitement, right? Making time for sex should be something you can discuss openly with your spouse. No matter how many years you have been married, we need to focus on keeping the spark lit. Naturally, as the years pass your sexual relationship changes. This happens for many reasons, one being hormone/age related changes and also a person's libido. How often you make love with your spouse is personal to you. What you need to work on continually is when you are going to make time for intimacy and sex. If you are the primary care giver of young children, try to have some time alone from when the kids go to bed to turn your mind to being intimate with your partner. It is tough to switch our mind instantly from one role to another. We need a little foreplay of the mind to get us there. You may draw a long bath for yourself, practice some simple deep breathing techniques, or ask for a foot massage or something that will allow you to turn your mind from children and chores to sex, intimacy, and love.

Some of us are romantics and wear our heart on our sleeves, and we have no problem showing affection and asking our partner for what we want. But there are some who find that behavior out of their comfort zone. People can feel afraid that if they express themselves, they will be rejected. It may be that they were raised in a way that they did not witness or receive a lot of affection as a child growing up. They may not know themselves well enough to know what they need, let alone ask their partners to give them what they need. Then there is the crystal ball theory of 'of course he/she knows what I want!' Whatever the reason, have patience and continue to show affection to each other. No matter how many years you have been married, it doesn't matter. To have a warm and loving marriage that is balanced, we need connection with touch. Explain to them how good it makes you feel when they love you up. Eventually, with patience, you should see some things change. If you feel you and your spouse have lost touch physically and emotionally over the years, seek help. If you were sick, you'd seek a doctor's help to find a solution, wouldn't you? Then why would your intimate and sexual health be any different? Never be embarrassed or too proud to work with a professional couple's counselor. There are many services within the military that offer this type of support.

Below are some suggestions to help you build affection with each other.

Could You Please

If we want something from our spouse, we have to ask for it. After all, they do not mind read! For some people, this is very difficult to do. And when we do not ask for what we want from our partner, we are left feeling frustrated and upset with them. There are specific ways to ask for what you want. This is important to address. If we are not tactful in our approach of asking, it can come across as an accusation.

Here is an example:

Scenario

I would like my husband to cook dinner on Saturday nights.

If I ask with the approach of, "You need to cook dinner this weekend," it comes across as an accusation like, "He never cooks dinner and that I'm tired of doing it."

The approach of "Would you mind helping me out by cooking dinner on Saturday nights?" is a more thoughtful, forthcoming way of asking.

Do you see how each scenario brings with it a picture of what is going on for the person asking and receiving the information? I would like you to begin practicing this task. You may be asking them for help with a physical task such as chores around the home or driving the kids to an after school activity. Or it could be something emotional, such as physical affection, a hug, a kiss, touch. Whatever it is you have identified with as needing more of, begin asking for it. In return, you must ask your spouse what they need. This seems so basic, but simple can be powerful.

Checking In

We get so busy with life events that we forget to check in with our spouses and see how each other's day went or what is on their mind. Make time to do this regularly. Don't allow this to be a 'honey do list' time or a bickering match. Choose a time and a place where you can be alone and take 5 or 10 minutes every day to talk and connect and see what's new with them. Maybe you do this in the evening when the kids have gone to bed or in the morning over a cup of coffee. Checking in every day sounds easy enough, right? When you work on this skill, look into each other's eyes so you both feel the connection. Pause before you respond to their thoughts or concerns; this shows you are present and considering a thoughtful answer. Don't interrupt until they have finished talking no matter how hard this may be!

Can I Ask You Out...

Date night, What's that? I hear some of you ask. If you cannot remember the last time you had a date with your spouse, it's been too long! This is the *5 Power Areas* of *Connection* and *Play*. Schedule a time and put it on your calendar. If you have children, schedule a babysitter or offer to trade with your friends.

    Don't allow cancellations, unless someone is sick. Stick with the appointment you have with each other to connect. The date does not have to be dinner. You may go for a hike or run together followed by breakfast. You may wander an art gallery. Try not to make this a movie date, simply because in the movie theatre your focus is on the screen and not each other. When you are on your date, do not allow yourselves to be on social media or using your phone in any way. When you are on your phone, you are taking away your attention from the real world and putting your energy into another reality. This can be very frustrating, and it sends the wrong message to your partner. Some people's jobs do not allow them to turn off their phones, but try hard to minimize its use. The importance of dates is to rekindle the 'just the two of you' part of your relationship minus the daily drama of your lives. Just practice having fun and making a connection. Often I find clients underestimate the importance of reconnecting with their partner. Before there were the stresses of life and you were newly married or dating, think about all the fun and laughs you had. Reflect on how you paid close attention to what the other was saying. You gave each other space, time and respect. In our hurried lives, we often forget this simple yet powerful act. Dates will help rekindle what may be lost.

Wine Me and Dine Me

Who doesn't want some romance in their lives? Whether you make a romantic meal for your spouse complete with candles, cook together, drink a great bottle of wine and listen to soothing music in a candlelit room, cozy up on the couch in front of the fire, or take a bath or shower together, take time to play and reconnect just like newlyweds. Some of you may want to have a glamorous night out on the town, so get dressed up and go out for the evening. Whatever appeals to you, schedule the time and make it happen. Your relationship is worth it.

Vacation Time

When was the last time you and your spouse took time away together? If you can afford to take a weekend away, go for it. You may need to leave your kids with friends or hire a babysitter. If you have friends or family coming to visit, consider asking them if they will watch your children for a night so you can get away. Your family will relish the opportunity to be with your kids and spoil them. You both get to return having had a mini honeymoon, a little more refreshed and ready to play hostess. It will take some organizing, but it will be worth it. If you cannot afford to go away, maybe you stay in your home but you send your kids for an overnight or two to a friend's house, and you return the favor for them. Then create some special times together, do a tourist activity in your hometown, watch a movie at home, sleep in, take an afternoon nap complete with massages. Get creative and enjoy each other! Escaping your reality and connecting with your spouse is a powerful tool in relationship building.

Connecting to your Spouse's Career but not Wearing the Rank!

Have you ever asked a friend what their spouse's job is? This is a tricky question as they often have jobs that change completely from one year to the next! However, sometimes you will get a definitive answer, other times a shrug of the shoulders and a response that's something like this: "Hmm, it's confusing. It involves ships, and that's all I can tell you!" I'm simplifying here, but you get my drift. Could you tell me today what your spouse's job entails? I am not asking you to be able to be able to give a slide point presentation of every detail or talk in acronyms; heavens knows there are hundreds of those! I'm suggesting you just try to grasp the basics of their job. The reason being is it shows that you are interested in what they do and that you support them. Imagine how you would feel if someone asked your partner to describe what you do for work outside the home or in the home, or what kind of a parent you are, but all they could come up with was a wishy washy answer. How would that make you feel? Unimportant, that you don't matter? That you possibly don't work too hard? Work together with your spouse by building an open communication to talk and listen to each other. We all deserve to feel appreciated. Make a point today to ask your spouse how their day went and what they were working on, and in turn ask them to give you the space to share your day with them.

    Throughout our military journey, we meet all kinds of people. There are those who have a tremendous amount of knowledge about their spouse's job and the military in general. These people know a lot not only about their spouse's job and who works for their spouse but also with their spouse. They have a wealth of information because they have put time into learning about how it all works. This is admirable if it is used to the advantage of the community in finding answers for questions someone may have. However, it has come to my attention with over twenty years of observation that sometimes some people can get so wrapped up in all of this information that they forget they are the spouse and not the active duty member. Be proud of your spouse and their job and support them, even brag about all their hard work and commitment to the military, but don't wear their rank. Did I just say that out loud? I sure did! As the spouse of a military member in a military community, we are in charge of no one but ourselves. We are not superior in any way to anyone else! We all deserve to be treated equally with respect and dignity.

I am not here to hurt anyone's feelings or undermine what their spouse does for work. Everyone has a major role to play. Our spouses all have an important job that helps their boss, their team, their commander in chief and the U.S. Military. I understand there are hierarchies and differences between the active duty members' rank and position with both the officers and the enlisted community. Notice I said differences between the active duty members. But to us, the spouses, it only means a difference in job titles and experience. No matter what rank your spouse wears or what job they do, we are all people at the end of the day. We wake up in the morning and pull our pants on one leg at a time just like everyone else! If we were to meet in life outside of the military in a social setting, would it matter what rank your spouse was or the job they did? Naturally, we will always respect each and every person's service to our great country and the sacrifices made. But would you choose not to interact with that person because of the position or rank they once had? I doubt that very much. Put your focus on building friendships with people who you find fun, interesting and engaging. Be with people who uplift, comfort and support you and leave the drama behind.

 Being a military family is more than a set of orders, packing up your home into boxes, transferring your kids to another school and starting life over again. It is about honor, sacrifice, and commitment for all of us, not just the active duty member who is serving. We are all serving. We are all doing our part to support the U.S. Military. It requires courage to see our partner leave on deployments. It requires patience to live with the unknown and strength to see the journey through to the end whenever that time comes for you and your family. You are a part of that big, crazy, adventure-filled military world. Embracing life's journey humbly is the ideal way to live a fulfilled life with a transient lifestyle.

The Dreaded D Word... Deployments

In the world in which we live today, deployments are long and worrisome. Way back in the early days of my marriage, deployments were 5 or 6 months in duration. Now when we say goodbye to our loved ones we are looking at much longer separations. This takes a toll on everyone. It is vital that you are always building a life of your own, as I discussed earlier. This is important all the time, not just during times of separation. When you have your own interests, hobbies, and friends you have a support network and an exciting life that keeps you moving along and not just at home feeling depressed. I am a cyclist and love to ride my bike. Every Saturday morning my husband had a scheduled babysitter, and we would take off and ride our bikes together. That usually ended at a coffee shop for a delicious pastry and a cup of tea! I continued with this when he deployed, riding every weekend with friends. It was a great workout, and it saved my sanity! I challenged myself to complete an organized century ride! Not only did I make it to the end, but I also had fun, and I felt so proud of myself and knew my husband would be proud of me too. Riding my bike gave me that much needed mental break away from my kids and everyday worries.

What could you do during deployments that would give you a mental break? Make time every week to take a mini sanity break. You may go to a book shop, walk in the park or attend a yoga class. Whatever ideas you come up with, work out a plan to make them happen and mark it on your calendar. Even just getting your kids to bed an hour earlier than usual one evening a week would give you a little 'you' time.

      Clients ask me what they can do to mentally prepare for deployment, how to keep the love alive while their spouse is gone and how to reunite. I could probably write a book on this alone! Here are some of my thoughts. When you look back to the *5 Power Areas* diagram and the *4 Cornerstones* diagram, you will be able to see the word *Connection* with these areas and how it relates to deployment. The first thing we have to do is practice acceptance. The deployment will come, and we cannot do anything to stop it. No amount of arguing and fighting will help. It's going to happen, and we should focus on building our relationship before our separation, not destroying it. Next is change; we need to focus on how we are going to accept the changes that come with deployment. What do you see as changing, what areas of your life will change during this time? You may recognize that you will be a temporary single parent, or you may have lost your one and only friend. You may be wondering what you will do every evening if you have no children at home. Whatever it is that you can identify as changing, first accept it and next come up with some simple solutions that could help.

Seek help from friends, and if they offer to help take it graciously. Get out and socialize. This could be with other parents, friends or colleagues. Attend some of the social events that your spouse's command will hold. You will be surrounded by people who feel just like you. Even if it is out of your comfort zone, push past it and recognize it will save your sanity and your health. Trade up kids with other parents and get some downtime. You could use the time alone to relax at home or go out and do something fun. You may choose to break up the deployment by visiting family if possible. One of the things I found helpful during my last deployment was at the end of every month, one month closer to homecoming, I would have a celebration. I choose to do this by popping the cork on a bottle of champagne or a great wine! I shared it with a friend, or if my family was visiting, I'd celebrate with them. I can tell you I had 11 corks by the end of the deployment! I'd also celebrate with my kids; we'd do something special like a trip to Lego Land or the movies and dinner, and sometimes we'd bake a celebration cake. We'd do something we would not ordinarily do in our day to day lives.

These small life events help you to keep an upbeat attitude.

Practice Flexibility; nothing is perfect. You may write an email and not hear back for some time. That happens when spouses are deployed for various work related reasons. Your spouse may get an extension. No, this is not ideal, but sometimes due to unforeseen occurrences, they have to stay 'out there' longer. This is a difficult situation, but the sooner we get on board with Acceptance and Flexibility, the easier time we will have trying to get our heads around the new situation.

Show Empathy for your spouse and yourself. No one is getting an easy deal here; you both have your challenges. It's not a contest to see who has the raw end of the stick. Deployment is a challenging part of military life, and unfortunately there is no way of backing out of it. We have to learn ways to not only cope but continue to live a full life. Give Gratitude for the fantastic partner you have, who is deployed and fighting for our freedom. They are making just as many sacrifices as you are to ensure our world is a safer place.

Deployment Exercise

Identify one of your biggest challenges you have experienced when your spouse was deployed. If you have not been through a deployment, think about something that concerns you about the upcoming deployment. Using action steps, come up with three solutions for each concern you have that could change that situation or thought.

Together but apart...

Trying to keep a stable connection while being separated from the love of your life is no easy task. The most important advice I can offer is to be open and honest. Some spouses put on their happy face even if things are going downhill at a rapid clip. They don't think it is OK to say how they are truly feeling. It's taboo! I have witnessed spouses hiding many things that were weighing on their mind for the sake of the deployed spouse. Naturally, we don't always want to get on a Skype call or send an email complaining and moaning about how life is not fair. But if you truly are feeling sad, lonely or you are dealing with a situation you'd like a little clarity on, please share it with your spouse. If they were at home, they'd want to help, right? So why would that change because they are deployed? Don't play the martyr card; no one expects you to be everything and do everything alone. Be real and be open and true to yourself.

    It will keep you connected. I believe for a relationship to continue to be supportive and grow we need to nurture each other in the bad times and the good. If you are having a bad day, express that you are asking for help and a virtual hug. That's all part of your relationship. They, in turn, will want to vent their frustrations; give and take is essential. Keep an open space for them to talk and you will receive the same.

    Give gratitude for the mere fact that we no longer live in a world where we are relying solely on snail mail back and forth between families. When I was first dating my husband and he deployed, it was during the time email was just coming onto ships. Heck, email was just coming into our homes! I'd send an email or two, and the replies would come back all jumbled up! I'd receive what seemed like cryptic messages that did not match the message I had sent. I guess at that time they had to be downloaded onto some kind of server? It is amazing today that we can get a message to our loved one while deployed so quickly. We can Face Time or Skype; some fathers even witness their wives giving birth while they are thousands of miles apart. I am always in awe of ladies who have had to bring a life into the world without their spouse - that's bravery and independence!

The one area clients fall short on ideas is how to handle intimacy during deployment. We must address this, as it is a part of our biology to want to express touch. When your spouse is deployed, it's true that our cup does not runneth over with great sex! But we still need to create an intimate connection. You need to get creative in thinking of ways to send touch, hugs, and love across the miles, and there are many ways that spouses do this.

Here are a few examples to keep the connection alive.

- Send creative care packages.
- Have a Skype dinner date, eat a meal together and connect.
- Write each other love letters using snail mail.
- Journal for each other - send them on deployment with a journal and write to each other and send a photo of the pages daily if you can.
- Get non-risqué professional photos taken of yourself looking sexy and beautiful - but not something that will get your partner in trouble!

- Make playlists and share them with your spouse. It could be music that has a memory attached to it. Load up an iPod with music to give before your spouse leaves.
- Read a daily devotional to each other.
- Consider reading "The Five Love Languages Military Edition" by Gary Chapman. You could discuss your thoughts via email or webcam.
- Check on sites like Pinterest for other ideas to get your creative juices flowing.

Homecoming!

Yes, the deployment is over, and you are on the final countdown to the big celebration! You've cleaned the house right down to each window blind and baseboard. You've planned out all your spouse's favorite meals that you will cook. The kids have made posters and banners that they are hanging with pride all over the exterior of the house. You've even picked out that special outfit to wear. Your heart is about to burst with excitement! There is no better feeling in the world than this special day. I can never stay dry eyed when I witness a homecoming, even when it has no personal connection to me other than I know how it feels and can relate to the experience. It is a time of excitement, but for some it can cause anxiety.

Client's Deployment Story

> *After many deployments, I could feel my resentment building up inside. When my husband came home after months away, he'd want things to go back to his way of doing business. I'd get frustrated; we'd argue a lot. I'd been doing just fine without his ways. Why should I feel the need to change back to his way now? I've had to take care of a toddler, our baby and worked part time with no help. I've had to hold it all together by myself. Don't tell me how to be a parent or how to run our home when you are never here.*

Sadly this is not a unique story. But as a health and lifestyle coach, I read between the lines here, and I can see there is more going on than just the frustration of the husband who returned and wants answers to questions. There are anger and resentment here too. There is also the ability to see that this person had no support network in place. That they never came up with goals together and outlined who would do what and how things would be done. There was a lack of conversations and connection. It is no wonder she was feeling bitter, exhausted and lonely; this makes me so sad. If we connect regularly and we hear each other's concerns, we can come up with solutions. Talking is essential, and again seeking professional help may be needed.

Reintegration has a honeymoon period. At first, everything is new and fresh again, and love is in the air. For some, it remains that way for the most part, and the deployed spouse returns and slides right back into whatever is going on in their home. That's a lucky family who can pick up where they left off. But it doesn't just happen by chance. It happens this way for some and not for others due to personality types. Some people are more placid than others and just fly by the seat of their pants; it's just who they are. But also the couples who can slide back into everyday routines after deployment can do this because they have built an understanding with each other and expectations of each other in their relationship. They are working on this life skill together all the time, not just in preparation for deployment. They work on finding common ground with what they both need and want. The boat gets rocky when the spouse who returns would like to have things their way. They want things to go back to the way they were before deployment. The spouse who was home *holding down the fort* feels resentment and frustration, and things can become very heated. To try to avoid this or a similar situation, we need to look to resolve it before it even has the chance to rear its ugly head. In our military community, there are many courses on offer to help with this. Having conversations with each other and setting boundaries, goals and expectations with each other is key. We need to hear each other out, respect where we are each coming from, listen to one another and find the common ground of agreement. These conversations have to happen regularly for this to work. Again, seek professional help if you need guidance in this area of your relationship.

Today, it is common for spouses who return from deployment to experience PTSD, post-traumatic stress disorder. If you observe this in your partner, please seek professional help as both a couple and individually. You cannot work through this alone.

My Homecoming Story

My husband had been deployed for close to 11 months. I was so excited for his return, and it was everything I had hoped for and more. During deployment, we had discussed the idea of just the two of us taking a couple of nights away together. After playing the role of a single parent for such a long time, I desperately needed to escape my young children. Of course, I loved them, and they were great company for me when my husband was deployed, but I needed a break! On the flip side, my husband who had not seen the kids for such a long time did not want to leave them just yet. He did not share my eagerness to leave. This was understandable, but he did not hear my needs. So one day about three weeks after homecoming I had reached my mental mom limit capacity! I had to get away. So that's what I did. With no plan in mind, I left my husband to spoil the kids and dote on them as much as he wanted and drove only 50 miles away, booked into a hotel and sat alone eating pizza, watching movies and drinking red wine. It was glorious! During the day I'd walk the beach and use the time to reflect and have fun shopping in my favorite consignment stores. I was only gone for two nights, but it was just what I needed! My moral of the story is to listen to what your gut is telling you and make it happen. I knew my husband understood my need to escape the kids and he supported me.

Exercise 10
Spouse Connection

Look at your 5 Power Area mind maps that you made earlier. Focus on the Connection mind map. What ideas and thoughts came up for you there? Pick 1-3 ideas that appeal to you and come up with some action steps to help you turn your relationship dreams with your spouse into a reality. This does not have to be a big, grand scheme. It may be as simple as scheduling a regular night in to share a glass of wine with your spouse and talk. Or planning a date night or building more intimacy into your week.

Your Family Connection

When we think of the word family, we may bring up an image in our mind of a 2.2 family—a white picket fenced home and a dog. The fairy tale image, right? If only life were that simple. Families come in all shapes and forms today. We have the nuclear family with the two parents and their children, there are blended families with stepchildren and stepparents, there are mixed race and religion families, and lastly there are our extended families, parents, in-laws, cousins, aunts, uncles, etc. The dynamics of family life are complex. As a military spouse, you are a part of one of these family types. But due to this transient lifestyle, I find that my clients often feel out of the loop. The sheer distance between themselves and their family can be challenging. I know this only too well—my family is now spread out over four continents! Clients express their concerns that they no longer feel that they are as close to individual family members as they once used to be due to the distance between them. Often a sibling in close vicinity becomes closer to their parents, and instead of feeling thankful that their family has this connection, sometimes this closeness stirs up resentment and jealousy. This is even more so profound if we are stationed at an overseas location. We are faced with many occurrences that agonize us because we cannot be there. We learn of family members who get sick or are in need of surgery; we miss out on many celebrations such as marriages, births, christenings, birthdays and so much more. Often due to expense and distance, it is not always possible to be physically there. When we are faced with realities such as these, instead of feeling sad by the experience, let's change our mindset and think about what we can do. What can we do right now today to feel better about the distance between our families and ourselves?

Here are a few ideas:

- Make the best family wall full of photographs that you love. I even put prints of photos in other places, like my jewelry box, in a book I'm reading, on a notice board, on a screen saver, etc.
- Get on the phone. Take advantage of the services out there that provide cheaper calling plans. I've used Vonage for years. It used to be 1cent a minute to the U.K. I could talk for an hour—it was the best $6 I've ever spent!
- Use the free calling App on What's App.
- Use Skype and FaceTime—the magic of being able to see family and not only hear their voices is truly the best gift we can be given.
- Send care packages.
- Write letters and ask for them to write back—receiving handwritten notes is extra special.
- Make photo books online. Giving and receiving this gift is a wonderful way to keep memories alive. My mother-in-law does this for me. She captures special events and gives the book to us as a gift. I treasure every book. It is fun to relive those precious memories with every turn of the page.

- Keep a family blog. I know many clients who do this, and everyone loves it.
- Keep Instagram and Facebook alive.
- Save up for a family visit or consider paying for a ticket for someone to come to you. It is often cheaper to do this than you paying for several tickets for your whole family to travel home.

Of course, nothing can replace the fact that you are far away from your family, and unfortunately that is just the reality of our lives as military spouses. What is important to remember is that your family does understand. They do not blame you; they are proud of you, always remember that. At some point no matter how hard it is to be separated from those we love, we have to accept it and do the best we can with the given situation. Look at the *4 Cornerstones of Life* diagram—*Acceptance, Empathy, Flexibility, And Change*—and understand how they relate to your separation from your family. At the end of the day, give gratitude that you have a family who loves you and one that you can turn to. If we don't work on the positives, the only thing you are left with is sadness. You owe it to yourself and your family to not allow yourself to dive into the depths of depression because you are far away. Be thankful for the things you can do and the times when you do get to be with your family. They will be even sweeter because you understand that the time is precious.

Find Your Tribe - The Friendship Connection

It is so important to make friends. It is essential for our emotional health. Having someone who you can depend upon and share your deepest thoughts with and have their support is priceless. Some people thrive on having many friends; others like to keep more intimate connections. What is important is to feel a connection to someone in your life whom you can call a good friend. This person should be someone who is supportive, encouraging, fun and trustworthy. The positive traits you find in your friends will be beneficial to your health and happiness. When you need guidance, they will be there for you. When you need a shoulder to cry on, they will be ready with the Kleenex, and you will be there for them in the same way as well. It is an important partnership that you are building together.

Be selective in picking your tribe; you do not want to surround yourself with people who will bring you down. You are familiar with these people I'm sure. They are the ones who complain about everything even when things in their life seem to be going OK for them. These types of people will drain your energy, and you don't need that. You need to be able to trust your friends. You may not want to share your life secrets with them, but there should still be a mutual respect and trust between you. If you feel in your gut that this is not the case, let this so-called friendship go without regret and don't beat yourself up over it. Accept that there are people in this world who are not genuine. Feel empathy for how challenging and lonely their life will be if they continue to play on people's heartstrings.

When you make friends, don't put all your eggs in one basket. What I mean by this is don't look for that one friend who has everything in common with you. Friendships don't always work like that. Don't worry about their age, their spouse's rank, their job, their religion or nationality, or any other stereotype when you are searching for your tribe. The beauty of friendships is what each person brings to the table. You may find a friend who loves to golf like you, or another who likes to eat at vegetarian restaurants, perhaps a friend who shares a passion for volunteer work. Who knows what type of friends you will make when you are open and do not peer down a telescopic lens trying to find the perfect match. Feel thankful that you have friends who fill the different niches of interest that you have.

It's true that as we get older it can be more challenging to make new friends. When we are younger, and especially if you have children, you are almost automatically built into a network of moms and dads because of your kid's school activities, playgroups, and other social events. But as your children grow up and leave home, it becomes more challenging. The most important piece of advice I can offer in this situation is to put yourself out there. It's just that simple.

One of my dearest friends I met in a gym off base. She had seen me working out and was essentially sizing me up for a Hawaiian outrigger paddling team. She asked me to a paddling practice; even to this day I am surprised I agreed to this as at that time in life I did not do anything related to sports and water. Water was my nemesis. My water limit back then was the shower! But I needed to make friends, so I felt the fear, stepped up to it and went out on a limb. I went to that practice and had to paddle the canoe—yikes! That was 21 years ago, and now my friend and I marvel at how funny it is that I am now her age when we met, her being 20 years my senior. Imagine if I had not put myself out there. I'd have lost out on an amazing friendship.

The moral of my story is you can find friends in all kinds of places if you're willing to put yourself out there. Today there are even more options with the many online groups such as MeetUp.com that have organized groups of likeminded people gathering for yoga, running, book clubs, hiking groups, cooking classes and crafty gatherings, etc., as well as all the offerings in your military community. If you explore, you are sure to find someone who you make a connection with. Please bear in mind that they were all new to the group once too. The difference is they were brave enough to be open to the possibility of what could come. Now it's your turn.

    Having military friends is great because they can relate to your life. They understand what your life is like because they are living the same life too! But sometimes we all need to escape our reality, right? That's when I find it helpful to have civilian friends too. Civilian friends are your safe zone. You can share with them anything about your military life, and you know that it is going to stay with them. They may not fully understand your military life, and that's OK. Civilian friends get those of you who may be too shy or get stuck in a rut with on base living to get off the base! You may be more likely to explore more opportunities in the place you are living with a civilian friend. The other beauty of finding civilian friends is they are less liable to be moving in a few months, and you won't be faced with saying goodbye unexpectedly. Plus if you go back to the same duty station, you'll already know someone. That is a huge win-win!

Exercise 11
Friend Connection

Look at your mind maps once again under the *5 Power Areas* of *Connection* and *Play*. What came up surrounding friendships within these areas? Do you want to meet up for a friends' night out once a month, or perhaps you want to find some new friends and are considering asking out some people at your yoga studio? Using the ideas that came up and keeping the big rocks theory in mind, plan some action steps and make time to build relationships with others.

Breaking Up is Always Hard to Do

We've all been there. We make the most lovely friends in each duty station only to have to say goodbye once again. It breaks our heart.

I had a friend who learned I was leaving soon and all of a sudden she stopped contacting me, she did not return my calls, and she didn't reach out to have grown up playdates or kids playdates. One day I called her on it, and she confessed that she always does this. "I just cannot bear saying goodbye," she said. Being the type of person I am (bossy my mum would call it!), I said, "Well that's a shame. I'm going to knock on your door, call your phone and offer to take your kids to the park. I'm not going to give up the last few months we have together because it's hard to say goodbye!" There were shared tears and then a realization on her part that she was not living an authentic life. She was hiding behind her fears, instead of facing them. She did eventually come around with some persuasion. But it certainly was not in her comfort zone to do so.

It happens to us all at some point or another; we get tired of saying "see you soon" when deep down inside we are wondering when that will be if ever. Sometimes we believe it is easier not to allow ourselves to become too involved with the people we meet because of the dread of the inevitable. I have heard clients describe their friendships as only face to face, and when they leave they are forgotten. Clients also describe how difficult it is to put their trust in new friendships.

I like to coach people on how to view their relationships differently. Take a moment to think about that one awesome friend you made in one of the places you lived. You know the one; you can finish each other's sentences, they are easy to be around, you clicked with them the first time you met. This is what I like to describe as a true companion. The saying you can count your true friends on one hand is a pretty accurate statement. This person you have in your mind right now is your confidante, your best bosom buddy. You trust this person with your life, your secrets, your fears and joys, everything. That is wonderful; celebrate the fact you have such a person in your life. They are always going to be there for you, even if they are not in your physical location. Please recognize this and tuck this sacred relationship in your heart. Naturally, we wish we could just pop over and see this person for a cup of coffee and a natter, and that is what is hard about leaving our best friends behind. But just knowing you have such person in your life who you can FaceTime with anytime is worth savoring and should bring you some peace.

Don't expect that every person you meet will become as good a friend as your one true best friend. You don't need every friendship you have to fill this ideal. Your other friendships will be more casual; there is nothing wrong with that. You are still your authentic self, but you can relax and not feel the need to catch this person up on all your life events. This new friend does not have to be your everything. Enjoy the friendship for wherever it is at. It may grow deeper; it may not. Just enjoy being present; stop worrying about where it is going. It's kind of like when you begin dating someone. Some people worry so much about where the relationship is leading they forget to live in the moment and just enjoy the experience. I'd also like you to recognize that to keep a friendship alive takes commitment. You have to work at staying in touch. You will know the people you will want to do this with, and you must make time in your schedule to do just that. Set up times to chat over FaceTime with a cup of coffee and catch up. Send them little care packages or snail mail letters. Friendships work both ways. Everyone has to make an effort, and you will never regret it. But what you will regret is not reaching out across the miles and losing touch. You remember earlier the story of my canoe paddling friend; we kept in touch over the years after I had left Hawaii. I did not get to see her again until we were stationed back in Hawaii 17 years later, and it was like no time had passed us by! We picked up where we left off sharing stories and having fun. The only thing that had changed was we are both gray and wrinkly!

References:

http://militaryspouse.com/relationships/civilian-friends/eight-ways-to-find-your-new-best-friends/

http://www.military.com/spouse/relationships/military-marriage/how-long-married-military-couples-stay-together.html

http://www.foryourmarriage.org/everymarriage/enrichment/sex-and-intimacy/

https://www.boldsky.com/relationship/love-and-romance/2014/twenty-reasons-why-physical-intimacy-is-important/articlecontent-pf66653-046481.html

*Through The Looking Glass - Lewis Carroll

Chapter 3

Ambition

When we think of the word ambition, we reflect on a desire to do something. We have an objective, we set ourselves goals, and we focus our attention on being successful. Ambition can be equated with many things in your life. Often people attach the word to work, career or education goals. But in reality you can have ambitions in many areas of your life. You may be someone who is striving to get fitter and run a marathon, so you have the goal of setting yourself up with a running/ walking program that will lead you to eventually running the race. Or perhaps you are a person who plays a musical instrument, and you have set a goal for practicing a classical piece of music and eventually learning it by heart with no sheet music. Or ever since being a teenager, you have wanted to visit the city of your dreams. Whatever ambitions you have, listen to them. Don't ignore them and think there is no way you can achieve your goal. As a military spouse, it is important to recognize that you can have a dream, you can be ambitious, and this transient lifestyle should not stop you from achieving that. You may have to get creative in achieving some of those dreams, and there may be some detours along the way. Accept this but keep moving forward. This is your one shot at living your best life, right? Why not create visions for your life and make them a reality.

Client story

I was coaching a seasoned military spouse; she'd lived the military lifestyle for 20 plus years. During her sessions, she talked about how she felt her life just rallied around her children; she had four kids ranging from 8-18 years. Her life consisted of cooking meals, cleaning, and driving kids to and from after school activities in 'mom's taxi.' She wasn't complaining; she was just sharing what we all experience, the challenges of raising a busy family in today's fast-paced life. Raising children is a priority for most parents, and providing a secure and stable environment for our children is very important. I believe there is no job as important as this. But when I asked her about her joy and where she finds pleasure, she drew a blank. The common excuse came up, "I'm waiting for the right time. This is just not my time right now."

I knew this client had a creative gift that she had been blessed with. She enjoyed refinishing furniture, and she was exceptionally good at it. She had not done this for quite some time. I suggested that she begin doing this again. We brainstormed a few ideas, set some goals together and from there my client began buying, refinishing and selling furniture to other spouses on the base and Craigslist! She also had the desire to learn how to re-

upholster furniture. She found a place where she volunteered her time while being mentored in how to hone in on this skill. Her hobbies had turned into her job. She set herself goals, a schedule, and apace that felt balanced. She took action. She had created a new dimension in her life and found solace that led to her happiness.

Here are the three simple steps that she took to change her dream into reality:

- Look at what I already know how to do and begin doing it again. She didn't try to reinvent the wheel!
- Find out how to do what I love and make money doing it.
- Learn a new craft and grow as a person.

Naturally, this approach does not fit everyone's ideal, but you can see how setting some simple goals and taking action led to her success. She was no longer filling her time with only the mundane tasks of daily living. Of course, she still had to do those things, but she had added a creative outlet that gave her a deeper sense of satisfaction. Naturally, she could have walked away from our conversation and stayed with the safe bet of 'my time to do something new will happen when my kids leave home' or another story. But she dared to dream and took a chance. She became a mini entrepreneur in her own right doing something she loved.

How Do I Keep Moving Forward with my Career and Education?

If I had the perfect answer for this question, I'd share it with the military world! I wish I had the perfect solution. How do we continue to thrive and make gains with our career and education choices when we are faced with so many challenges as a military spouse? Having a successful career or education path within the military lifestyle is a constant challenge for us all. It does not matter what job you have or what degree or masters program you are trying to complete, you are going to come across obstacles due to moving from state to state, across continents and countries. I know many spouses, myself included, that have had to reinvent themselves more than once with each military move. I hear your frustrations; I live them too. But in the words of Winston Churchill:

"Never give in,
Never give in,
Never give in."

Even when the going gets tough—and it will—and you cannot seem to get exactly what you want, you must not give in to the alternative. You must dig deep into your soul and examine what your life will look like on the alternate side, the side of 'I can't do this again'. This dark demon will swallow you up whole and leave you in the deepest place of despair and frustration. I know this because I have seen it with many clients. I have coached them out of this sad place. This place is not an option for someone who knows what they want and has the drive to create the life they dream of. This person is you; you have a robust and determined force— never forget that. You cannot expect things to change if you don't fight for what you want. Your next duty station may be no simpler solution to the place you are now, my point being don't wait for your circumstances to change; work with what you have. This is your life, and it's happening. Don't press pause on your dreams.

I know there are many of you reading this and rolling your eyes! You may be thinking not another pep talk! Some of you have degrees and once had a career in your trained field before you married your spouse. There are those of you who are hoping to get an education in a chosen career field so you can get a job. Lastly, there are some of you who opted to give up on your career to pursue your job in raising your children. Wherever you are in your ambition journey, you will need to stay flexible and get creative to make this work. I know spouses who want their own businesses, those who want to work in law firms, others who are nurses, teachers, graphic designers, artists, accountants and on and on it goes. The people who can keep working are the ones who have the drive to move forward with each move. They look dynamically in their job search and are flexible with their outlook.

I use the word flexible because we have to be realistic. I would be doing you a disservice, for example, if I led you down a path of believing that you could work at the same accounting firm for the rest of your military life. But you'd be doing yourself a disservice if you give up on a job opportunity in accounting because it does not fit your exact profile that you envisioned for yourself. I'd be doing you a disservice if I said of course you can own your clothing boutique business and never move it ever again. But you'll be dishonoring yourself if you don't allow yourself to begin building that dream and taking the steps you can in making some parts of it a reality until it can be the exact picture you want. You can apply this train of thought to any career field or education goal. When creativity is blended with the *4 Cornerstones of Life— Acceptance, Flexibility, Empathy And Change—* you can achieve results.

Finding the Work you Love

When you know you will be moving and that you will be looking for a job at your new duty station, as soon as possible start by updating your resume and if necessary getting some business cards made up. Then reach out to the power of the social media world. Let it help in connecting you to your network of friends. Let them know where you will be moving to and what type of work you are looking for. Be sure to let your friends know that the work doesn't have to be a perfect match to your ideal. When you post that you are looking for a job, be sure to include not only your profession but also any volunteer work you've done. Consider including your hobbies and interests. Who knows what may come out of it. Maybe you used to be a part time dog walker and your friend hears of a veterinary assistant job for which you could apply. Or perhaps you volunteered in your children's school, and they know of a teaching aid position that is available. Perhaps you used to work on the base at the ITT office, and you may now decide to look into hotels that offer booking services for activities for hotel guests.

Think about your interests, hobbies and your profession when you are looking for work both at home and outside of the home. You never know, all this exploring may lead you down a path of a new career discovery. The domino effect will run on and on in your favor if you get the word out there and do some homework. I'm hopeful that there will be someone out there who will be able to help you. The world is a small place when you begin reaching out to all your connections and them to theirs.

Don't look for perfection, rather find something that interests you and that you know would be beneficial to your work experience. Let go of putting your ideas into a perfect box. Think outside of the box and what you can offer.

Next, Google the area you are moving to and find all the companies, schools, etc. that provide employment you are looking for.

Be bold and send your resume to the businesses that appeal the most to you. Even if there is no vacancy open at present, get to know this company and them you. Follow up with a call to those companies and see if they received your resume. You could even go as far as to ask if you can meet in person and see their offices, etc. However you can make a connection is worth your time and effort. Being proactive in your job search will help you stay motivated.

Be flexible and realistic in looking for work. You may want a position in a law firm with a six figure salary, and one day I believe you will make that happen for yourself. The reality is as long as you are living a transient life you will need to live by the words give and take. You may find a job you would love, but it pays little in comparison to what you could be earning in other places or at another time in your life. You are now left with the option of not taking the job because it does not match your criteria or accepting the job because of the fulfillment it will bring you, giving you the opportunity to have an engaging and productive life. There is no perfect solution, but it is true to say that as a military spouse you will have to accept that you will need to make sacrifices. I want to make the following point very clear: making sacrifices does not mean giving up on your dreams. It just means you'll need to think a little differently on how you are going to get what you want. You may find that your situations vary depending on each duty location. In some places, you may need to start out with volunteer work or temp work to get your foot in the door with a company. You may even have to look for a job that is not in your field of work that you are trained in, but work that is available. In this situation consider the experience as a learning curve. You may be pleasantly surprised and find another career opportunity. The flip side of this coin is even though you may be considering taking work in an alternate career field, I would only recommend this if the work seems interesting to you. If it doesn't, move on and look for something else that appeals to you.

You are sure to find something if you continue to research. The only time you may be forced to take work that does not rock your boat is if you have exhausted all other possibilities and you are financially in a desperate situation where you need a second income pronto. When I talk about exhausting all other options, this is when the world becomes your oyster! Exhausting all possibilities when looking for work should be viewed in a very positive light. This is why.

    Let's use this scenario - you are a graphic designer and you cannot find full-time work. Be sure to look for temp work that could play out in your favor. Don't forget to search for online work, not just locally. In between temp jobs, look at what else is going on in your community, both on and off the base that interests you. Is there a link between your work ambitions and your hobbies? As a graphic designer, perhaps you have a desire to volunteer in a school teaching art class, or maybe you've dreamed of working in an art gallery or an art studio? Think big and broaden your outlook. You have incredible potential—use it. It's a gift given to you for a reason. Understand that the skills you are acquiring with the work you choose to take on will all work in your favor when you are applying for your next job whenever that is. It is much better to show your creative, flexible side to an employer rather than the person that gave up and sat at home watching afternoon television!

    I was building my personal training business out of our home alongside working as a personal trainer in a large fitness center in Northern Virginia. I was teaching all kinds of classes—Pilates, Spin, Bosu Circuits. I was also personal training clients and leading teams of people through a Biggest Loser type of program. I was working in a chiropractor's office with a friend teaching classes, and a dietician was just about to seek out my help in her business. I was doing the work I loved and earning a decent enough second income. Then our playing cards were dealt a different hand. We had to move from the booming metropolis of Northern Virginia to a small town of 5000 people in the Midwest an hour north of Green Bay. I'll never forget that day we drove into the town where we were to live, and I blinked and missed the whole thing! What on earth was I going to do for work here? Fitness was not a huge priority here. The community was blue collar, and personal training and Pilates were considered a luxury. There was, however, a very small YMCA. I approached them and offered my services. They could barely afford to pay me. I took a massive pay cut. I swallowed my pride and focused on what I could offer them and in return what I would get out of the experience. I helped begin their Spin program, I taught Pilates and Bosu classes, and even got some personal training and nutrition counseling clients. Sure, I made peanuts in comparison to what I could have earned. But it's not always about the money. I was able to provide this community a service and help to change their lives for the better. During those long, cold winters, I did not go stir crazy too often as I had a purpose, my work.

Exercise 12 - Career and Education

Using your 5 Powers mind map for Ambition, select 1-2 ideas about your career or education goals that you want to achieve. Then come up with some goals and assign some action steps for those goals using the example I described in chapter 1. Don't forget to put it on your calendar. Then you are turning your goals into a reality.

Online Work

The internet is fantastic! There are many resources available to military spouses to help you find employment. Military One Source is one of them. Seek out their help and let them guide you through your career options. They have experts who can support you. If you Google online work and military spouses in your search engine, lots of resources will pop up. There are large companies that actively seek out military spouses for employment such as At&t, Xerox, and Fed Ex just to name a few. The benefit of online work aside from the flexibility with your schedule is that they are often positions that are transferable.

Being able to find the work you love and be able to transfer it with you as you move is ideal. I knew a military spouse who had a dream of owning her own business. She also had a love of making jewelry, which was one of her hobbies. She married the two together, and voila she now has an online business designing, creating and selling jewelry. She also reaches out to the stores on the various bases that she lives, and she works with them to get her products sold locally. How inspirational is that? What hobby do you have that could be earning you an income?

You don't have to own your own business to have online work. You may offer a service. Although there are work-from-home jobs in practically every industry, the most sought after and most flexible jobs are in HR and recruiting, computer and IT, and education and training. If you brainstorm your options, you are sure to come up with some possibilities. For example, if you are a teacher but you don't want to re certify in the state you now live or at an overseas posting, you may consider tutoring or substitute teaching. Or if you are a bookkeeper you may take on your child's preschool bookkeeping tasks. This may blossom into private clients of the preschool parents who need an accountant for their business. There are also online businesses that offer opportunities in accounting and finance, travel and hospitality. Research your options and be open to all possibilities. Start by listing your skills and match them to your career, hobbies, and interests. You are sure to find something that interests not only you but also an area you can thrive in. I know this can be exhausting with each move, and I wish I had a magic wand to take the stress of this part of your life away; unfortunately, I don't. What I will advise is if you know yourself and that you will be happier working, you have to put in the time and effort no matter how tiresome this is. There is no alternative. If you value yourself and what you have to offer the world, then take a deep breath and put yourself out there.

You Have Value

Military spouses sell themselves short too often. Because they transition between jobs frequently, they consider this to be off-putting for some employees. Don't create an idea in your head about what a future employer may think in hiring a military spouse before you have even applied. Even if you have been turned down in the past, turn this thought process on its head. Look at all the skills you bring to the table that are unique to military spouses that are a huge benefit to all businesses. I could name a dozen right now, such as being able to work under pressure. Think about the stresses you see in your daily life and how you deal with them. You consider change a breeze; you adjust to many life changes that some people never have to face. You can work as a team player and build relationships quickly, can adapt to new work environments, work well independently or in groups, bring ideas from other companies to the new business, etc. Think about your lifestyle as an advantage for a prospective employer and sell them on it. The other thing to consider is if you have a specific profession, join the professional organization in your community that serves your field. Look into meet-ups in your area to connect with others who have similar interests, both personal and vocational. Be sure to hook up with networking groups and town hall-type meetings to familiarize yourself with what happens in the area. Lastly, check out the local chamber of commerce to find out who the top employers are and how they can help you and what you can offer them.

Education

In some duty locations, you may decide to pursue an education dream. You may be studying for an associates degree, a bachelors, masters, or Ph.D. or pursuing a vocational area of study—congratulations! How lucky are you to be able to continue learning and acquiring knowledge in your field of expertise or potential job field! When you are choosing a school to study at, if it is a physical school (rather than an online school), check to see if when you move you can continue with an online option of study or if they have campuses in other states that you may know could be a possible option for you and your family when the next move happens. Education is never lost. It will serve you well when the time comes for you to get a job in your desired field. But more than that, it is a way to stay engaged and focused and to feel productive in using your time well in the place you are now living.

    Online schooling is probably the best option for military spouses; it simplifies things. With online education being so prevalent, it opens up to a world of possibilities for military spouses today. In comparison to the way it was in the past, before the internet! I understand that there are challenges that come with continuing education and military moves, such as cost, transferable credits, relicensing costs in various states, and the sheer red tape with each process. Don't lose hope. Reach out to the many resources that can help you. The school you are attending may allow exceptions for military spouses with credit transfers, etc. and their continuing education credits. Military One Source and other base resources are also there to guide you through the process. There are many grants and scholarships to help pay for education expenses, along with the

GI Bill. Spend some time researching your options for financial help. If you don't reach out for what you want, you may be missing out on an opportunity. At the end of this chapter, I offer some website links you may be interested in researching. Your drive and ambition will lead to your completion and success.

Client Testimony

Oh, the 30-something blahs. As my friends and I were lamenting our concerns that our careers and other life goals weren't moving forward the way we'd all dreamed, a friend introduced me to Navenka. She quickly brought her upbeat and unbiased third party perspective to different areas of my life. Starting small, she helped identify areas I wanted to focus on, as well as areas I didn't realize were having a major impact on other areas of my life. Why wasn't I job searching enough? Why didn't I feel like I had time to work out in the mornings? Why was I always so sleepy? It was all connected. It's still a work in progress, but I got jolted out of my rut and ready to take action.

Resources:

Navy & Marine Corp Relief Society
http://www.nmcrs.org/locations

Coast Guard Mutual Assistance
http://www.cgmahq.org

Military scholarship finder
http://offers.military.com/v/scholarships/flow/

https://bluestarfam.org

www.victorymedia.com

www.hiremymom.com

http://militaryspouse.com/career/jobs-for-military-spouses/4-life-skills-that-translate-into-jobs-for-military-spouses/

https://www.voanews.com/a/military-spouses-battle-career-obstacles/2732129.html

http://www.military.com/education/money-for-school/military-spouse-and-family-educational-assistance-programs.html

http://www.workingmother.com/10-surprising-work-from-home-jobs-for-moms

http://www.military.com/education/keys-to-success/the-value-of-continuing-education.html

http://www.military.com/daily-news/2016/07/05/push-ease-licensing-military-spouses-remains-patchwork-state.html

Chapter 4

Play!

Are you having fun?

When we hear the word play, we often think of children. We understand the importance of play for children. We know it is a learning tool, a way for them to make friendships and build interactions with their peers. When you watch a child role play, you'll hear them take on a role as a mom or a dad or a teacher; they act out scenarios being creative, thoughtful and using their imaginations. How often do we get to release ourselves of our roles we work within day in and day out and take on a different persona? When can we stop being a grown up and just allow ourselves to have fun? As we grow older, play can be thought of as frivolous and time wasting. We live in our busy worlds, and as adults we forget to allow ourselves the time to play. We underestimate how much it can positively impact our lives. Think about your children or your friends' kids playing. There are squeals of excitement, belly rolling laughter, energy and great enthusiasm, right? When children play, they release pent up frustrations, and they are using their creative energy and relaxing. In turn, they are allowing all the wonderful endorphins to be released into their bodies.

Adults' bodies and minds also need to play, so we too may live a balanced, harmonious life. When adults play regularly, they are said to be more productive at work and around the home. Both our physical and emotional selves benefit from play; it can help boost your immunity and release anxiety and stress. It is not that adults who play are necessarily less stressed, but they are more able to let the worries of life roll off their backs with greater ease compared to their counterparts who play very little. Playing only on vacation alone is not enough. That amounts to very little fun time in the grander scheme of life.

When we do not engage in the gladdening of our hearts and making merry with ourselves and our friends, we become stuck in a funk; we get cranky, irritated and frustrated. Who wants to feel like that? Do you remember your childhood days when you'd go out to play with your friends? Hours would pass by, and you'd be so engaged in your activities you'd even forget to eat until your parents called you home for dinner. Those were great times, right?

Let's create some of what may be lost and put some playtime on your calendar. Yes, that's right, you have to schedule it in just like everything else.

This 5 Power Area of your life will not happen without you making time for it. Your idea of fun is unique to you. Some of you will seek out physical activities such as a Zumba class, dancing or rock climbing. Others may enjoy some lighthearted reading, a playful fairground ride, or watching your favorite comedian. Whatever it is you decide to do, let it warm your heart and lift your spirits. We all need to escape once in a while, and playing is the perfect way to do just that.

Exercise 13 - Physical Play

Look at your 5 Power Area mind maps that you made earlier. Focus on the Play mind map. What ideas and thoughts came up for you there? Pick 1-3 ideas for Physical Play that appeal to you, and come up with some action steps to help you make your play dreams a reality. This does not have to be a big, grand scheme. You may have a desire to play in the yard blowing bubbles with your kids! You may want to jump on your neighbor's trampoline! Or you may be thinking of taking regular family hikes. Your gut gave you a message; you need to act on it. No procrastinating—make it happen today by attaching your play ideas to dates and times and follow through.

Get Creative!

"I don't have a creative bone in my body!"

We've all witnessed someone saying this, maybe even ourselves. But it is not a true statement! We have all been given the gift of creativity; it is just that some of us are not sure what that gift is yet or how we can let that flower bloom. We've never allowed ourselves to explore this area of play. When we think of creativity, we tend to think of producing something like a piece of art, a one of a kind original! That is a lot of pressure to put on yourself! Look back to your early mind maps that you made and see what words and phrases came up around the 5 Power Area word Play and the connection it has to creativity. Some of your ideas may be bucket list items of things you've always wanted to try, but you have not been able to get the nerve up to experience it. Other thoughts you mapped out may be activities you are already engaged in but would like to get into more consistently or grow into a little deeper.

Exercise 14 - Creative Play

Again choosing the Play mind map, pick 1-3 ideas that appeal to you around *Creative Play*. Take the action steps needed for you to begin the creative craft you have in mind. Remember, when I say craft I use the term interchangeably with anything you find creative. It could be music, art, design, engineering, computer programming, making videos, scrapbooking, digitalizing all your photographs, solving Sudoku or coloring in one of those beautiful adult coloring books that are all the rage right now.

When we are creating, we have a constructive outlet that is healthy for our brain. We are filling up on our hopes, dreams, and desires. This outlet is a wonderful way to release tension and escape the monotony of daily life. Creating something that pleases you is vital to your emotional health.

I am a potter! There is nothing more relaxing for me than feeling a cold, smooth lump of clay in my hands and manipulating it into something beautiful. Sometimes I don't create anything that you can physically recognize. I am just playing with mud, having fun and leaving the reality of the world behind. Other days I create wonderful pieces of art that I enjoy giving as gifts. There is one amazing thing that happens when I am working on my pottery wheel; I can only live in the present moment. I cannot think of what is ahead or look back; my focus has to be present and on the ball of clay rotating around and around. Some days it is meditative, other days are more challenging.

Before I sit down at my wheel, I can usually tell what kind of an outcome I will have dependent upon my day. When I say outcome, I mean an object that resembles something! Even if I come away with a mass of clay that needs to be recycled, I have also come away with so much more—a moment in time that I could get out of my head and in touch with the moment. That is priceless. What could you do that will enable you to get out of your head?

What I have learned from my experience of creativity is it is all about the journey, not the outcome. The journey takes on a role of its own. It requires patience, persistence, imagination and a playful heart. Unless you are trying to earn a living from your craft, you need not worry about the outcome. Just enjoy the process. Remember your *4 Cornerstones of Life—Acceptance, Flexibility, Change And Empathy.*

By taking part in a creative activity, you will be a more content, fulfilled and happier person. You must let go of perfection. That is the enemy of creativity. Do you think the first time Van Goh painted a sunflower he had a million dollar painting? Nope!

I'm sure he worked his paint pallet and canvas many times over until he came up with what he decided was a keeper. But not everyone saw his work as ideal. That did not matter; he was happy with his masterpieces and the vision he had. Keep your eye on simplicity. If you are creating a piece of writing or a musical piece, don't overwork it. The great thing about being creative is the road never ends. You will change, grow and learn new things along the way. By keeping that open, organic concept, you will always find peace, success, and fun in what you are doing.

    Creativity can be channeled into many areas of your life such as work, sports, and your home environment. Some people have creative jobs; others have imaginative hobbies. Even your home environment can be a creative niche. There are many careers that exude creativity on a daily basis. Using your imagination in any number of ways at work requires you to be inventive, resourceful and inspired. Think about your job; does it allow you the opportunity to be these things? Remember, if you find it creative, then it is. There is no right or wrong answer here. Unfortunately, some jobs can stifle that side of your personality, hence the importance of having this window of opportunity outside of your workplace. If your job stifles your creativity, is it a good fit for you? Can you be happy working without fulfilling your own needs? We talked about finding the work you love in the chapter about ambition. I have coached many clients who have come to me in one job and rediscovered themselves only to find they had a second career inside of them that needed to be set free. Is this person you?

At home, you may be a very visual person and love to color outside the lines, but your work environment may not allow for that. As an outlet, you may go home in the evening and enjoy the act of creating art on a plate, combining spices, textures, and color in the meals you serve your family. Or it is possible you enjoy interior design and switching things around in your home, finding new places for new pieces of furniture or artwork. Maybe you'd enjoy helping friends with their homes? Could this be a side business? You may enjoy gardening and experimenting with pops of color with your plants and flowers. Could you start your own above ground vegetable beds? Is there work in a garden center you may enjoy? As a military spouse, if this is something you enjoy, you certainly get many opportunities to design different homes and gardens with each move you make!

If you are someone who has a type A personality and finds it hard to sit still and focus on a set task, perhaps you set yourself free with a creative sport such as dance, martial arts or geocaching. Maybe you need to be physically creative. Look at your options for other activities that offer this such as Zumba, Ariel yoga, kite flying, sea glass hunting or drama like maybe being part of a play or a musical. Keep your options open and explore your local community. Find out what is on offer that appeals to you.

Hobbies Can Help!

One of the many beautiful things about having a creative outlet and a hobby is the opportunities that open up for you in other areas of your life. When everything changes in your life, with your military moves and careers and your spouse's job, and you find yourself living in the place of the unknown once again, if you have a hobby, a creative outlet, you have something dependable in your life. No matter where you move to, this one thing that you love to do will always be there for you. You can count on it not changing. With this hobby comes a built in tribe of friends. You will meet people who share your interests. That should bring you some peace and comfort. Whenever I move, unfortunately I cannot pack my pottery wheel in my suitcase and not even in my express ship, but I can take a small selection of my ceramic tools with me. Then upon arriving at my new home or even before, I scout out places I can go to try a class and get my hands on some clay while I am waiting for my wheel to arrive.

Moving is said to be one of the most stressful things we do in our lives. Imagine having an outlet with your hobby for all the pent up frustration and anxiety that coexist when we find ourselves moving homes. Imagine if you'd packed your guitar and some sheet music or your sketch pad and pencils. You may say, "Oh, I don't have time. I'll be unpacking boxes and organizing one thing and the other." But let me ask you this: How long can you keep up that pace? Don't you send your kids out to play in the middle of the moving chaos? If they get to play and let off steam, why don't you? When your next move happens, allow yourself time to play and create. Use it as a reward for working hard. You may decide to work on boxes and unpacking for a few hours and then allow yourself an hour of free time. For this to happen, you will need to organize what you will need ahead of time, and if possible take what you need with you in your suitcase so that you have no excuses on the other end. Finding balance in all you do is the key to living a harmonious and purpose driven life.

Naturally, when you have a creative outlet, it is likely you can meet other people with a similar interest. When you seek out places to create and play, you will make new friends. It's a win-win for you, your health and the amazing people you will meet. If you find that your creative hobby keeps you at home because it tends to be a solitary activity, consider taking a class or short course that will enhance your skills and get you out of the house and meeting others. Many community centers and local colleges offer these types of activities; you can also search on meetup.com. They have a group for almost every interest out there!

Get Goofy!

> *"People shouldn't be embarrassed just because they get caught acting a little silly."*
> *Charles Shultz*

As we grow older, we forget to be silly and act a little crazy and goofy! Some people feel embarrassed behaving in such a way. We worry what others may think. We should learn to let go of these concerns and feel a pure joy that fills our hearts when we act silly! I love to chase my kids around the house at the same time we are pulling funny faces with each other. Then there are tickle battles or water hoses that just happen to have a mind of their own instead of pointing at the car to be washed! Even the dog and I get into it; I love to suck the helium out of balloons and talk to the dog, who completely loses it as we chase each other around the dining room table! Sometimes there are dance offs and jokes or April foolery in another month. What I know is laughing is an excellent medicine. When we laugh, we reduce our stress hormones cortisol and adrenaline, and we increase our endorphins and boost our immunity. When we relax and laugh, we lower our blood pressure. All these benefits and not a single adverse side effect. Being playful for some people does not come as easily, especially as we age, generally because we have more worries in our lives and responsibilities. But no matter what, I know we all need to work on this more. Can you get goofy today just for the sheer heck of it? The next time you take your kids to the pool, get in the water and have some fun splashing around and canon balling. If you're at the playground, play on the swings. How high can you go? Can you get to the point where you feel like you have a family of butterflies in your stomach? Play on the slide. How fast can you go? Can you slide on your belly or your back, head first maybe?! If you're at home, pull some pranks on your kids or your spouse—why not? Get wild once in a while. Let's all lighten up!

References:

http://www.smh.com.au/lifestyle/health-and-wellbeing/wellbeing/play-is-important-for-adults-too-20170521-gw9ysw.html

https://goodmenproject.com/featured-content/7-habits-that-foster-creativity-find-your-creative-genius-kcon/

Chapter 5

Inner Peace

Sit quietly for a moment and close your eyes. Take a couple of long, deep breaths and imagine your life with more peace. What does peace mean to you? It looks very different for many people. How do you find peace in your daily life? Or maybe you don't know how to. In this chapter, we will explore this *5 Power Area*.

What I come across time and again when I'm coaching is clients who are always giving, giving and giving some more. They give to their children, their spouse, their family, and friends. When I ask them, "Who is filling up your gas tank?" there is a blank stare looking back at me and sometimes tears just because of the relief that somebody else recognizes the situation. It is admirable to be a caregiver to all the people in our lives, but to be the best we can be in all the different roles we have, we must take care of ourselves first. For some people, this feels like entirely selfish behavior, and others simply don't know how to take care of themselves. It is not something we are taught or talk about. Think about when you are socializing with friends or family. We often discuss what we've been doing at work or the chores to be done. How often can you recall someone asking you what you are doing to relax and take care of yourself? A counselor once asked me, "When do you do nothing?" My reaction was, "Huh? Nothing, please define nothing. Do you mean reading a book, doing some yoga or watching T.V.?"

No, the question my counselor was asking me was when do I let my brain rest and sit and daydream! Back then in my early 30's, this was unknown territory for me. Rest, such a waste of my time! That was my mindset! Today if I had to answer this question I'd have a very different answer. Together we are going to explore ways that you can bring more peace into your life and how to master the art of doing nothing. Let me add, if you are like me and you have a type A personality, happily always on the move, this may be one of the hardest things to master!

People often associate quiet times with boredom. We have become a nation of doers. We are always doing something or going somewhere. The notion is if we are doing something outside of the home we are having more fun or being more productive. I am not sure I entirely agree with this concept. When we are not doing for ourselves, we are ushering kids from place to place, activity to activity. This can be exhausting. Of course, we are all busy, and we cannot avoid the activities of daily life. But we must find peace on a daily basis in a way that works for us and our lifestyle. This is important as it will help to counterbalance the business. I know families who achieve this by having family time where they do not allow friends to come over and they focus on being a family unit. Everyone just hangs around at home relaxing, maybe playing games together or taking a walk together around the neighborhood. Our homes are our security, our cocoons in life where we can regenerate our vital energy and emotional resilience.

    I'll come back once again to the way we raise our children; most parents raise their kids with some form of quiet time whether that's a nap or reading a book or spending time alone in their room playing quietly. Why did we think it was a good idea to stop doing this? Yes, we have busy jobs and family responsibilities, but there are 24 hours in a day. We need to create calm and restfulness other than when we are sleeping. You can miss a lot if you never slow down.

> *"A happy life must be to a great extent a quiet life, for it is only in an atmosphere of quiet that true joy can live."*
> *- Bertrand Russell*

Self-Care

To help you develop a habit of making time for regenerating energy and regrouping your thoughts of daily life, I will give you some different ideas that you can try in the area of self-care. Please allow yourself to put time and energy into you and what you need. Make yourself a priority—trust me, you will not regret it. By prioritizing yourself, you will see how your life evens out in other areas, bringing you more harmony. I want you to take a moment to slow down every day for at least one of the self-care ideas that I will share with you. If you are not engaging in one of these practices regularly, you are not mastering the art of self-care. Think of other habits that you have developed in your life; it took time for them to become a part of your daily life. The place of loving yourself up a little may be alien to you, but if you stick with it and consistently turn up for the work to be done, you will be a much calmer, more relaxed and happier person. Someone with a more positive outlook on life.

Meditation

There are many types of meditation. There are silent, guided and visual imagery meditations. People who find sitting through meditations a challenge can engage in physical meditations such as walking and running meditations. If you practice a mind-body exercise routine such as Pilates, tai chi or yoga, you will be pursuing some form of meditation in your class. These types of exercises focus on breathing techniques and imagery, which are part of most meditation practices. What works for some is not always a good fit for another person. Try on the different types of meditations for size and see which is a good fit for you. Don't be surprised if one day you need one type of practice and another day something different. That is normal; go with the flow and accept what your body is telling you that you need. If you are new to meditation, I recommend you begin with a guided form of reflection.

Guided meditations involve a person talking you through some images or helping you to create pictures from your past life stories in your mind. Your teacher will also help you to focus on breathing techniques, paying attention to pace and the length of each breath. They will also address the areas of your body they want you to breathe into. The idea behind guided imagery meditation is to help you stay focused and to be in the moment.

Silent meditation can be a little more challenging for the novice meditator, primarily because of the monkey mind playground your brain creates! Are you familiar with this place? You begin in earnest breathing and quieting the mind; you are repeating your mantra silently, and then all of a sudden you are off track and thinking about your to do list, or recreating a memory that happened earlier that day. Before you know it you've lost your groove, and you give up. Is this you? If so, don't lose heart. This is common and expected. It is virtually impossible to turn off the brain. The most important thing to learn is how to train those monkeys! When your thoughts wander off, bring them back to the sensation of your breath. This takes time, so have patience. Even the most committed gurus who have this practice down pat will at times experience monkeys at play when they sit on their meditation mat. There are some excellent apps out there to help the beginner, so check some out. One tip that I find useful is to listen to meditations wearing a headset. It helps to drown out environmental noise pollution and focus your mind.

The imagery in a meditation practice can be very helpful but also soothing. You may draw upon an experience in your life, a time or a place you felt completely at ease. You may visualize the waves of the ocean lapping up on a sandy beach that you once walked or the green pastures of a flower-filled field. It may be peaceful for you just to envision your favorite color and bathe your mind in it. Whatever helps you to stay in the moment is the ultimate goal.

Walking and running meditations are similar to seated meditations except for the fact that you are moving. It can be helpful for some people who perhaps have difficulty sitting still—remember the type A peeps? The pace of this kind of practice is languid and controlled. You will not be moving your body at your usual walking or running speed. However, it may help those who struggle to stay in one posture for any length of time. You will be bringing awareness to the muscles and the bones in your body and connecting the feeling of the earth under your feet to the actions of the body and breath. This discipline will take practice, eventually making it easier. There is a lot to distract you when you are outside like nature, neighbors, noise, etc., so perhaps begin with a guided version of this meditation to ease into it and help you keep your focus.

Exercise 15 - A Basic Meditation

Remember earlier we talked about gratitude being the glue of life that holds everything together? I'd like you to use this thought like a mantra and practice a short meditation. Find a quiet place to sit or lay down. Set a timer on your phone for three minutes and repeat the following mantra to yourself silently over and over again.

"I am grateful."

If your monkey mind comes to play, recognize they are just thoughts, hold no attachment to them, watch them drift away on a cloud, and come back to repeating the mantra. At the end of the three minutes, observe how you feel. What is different? How did it go—easy, hard or impossible? Wherever you are at is great. It is where you are supposed to be. Practice makes everything easier.

Consider making meditation part of your daily routine. You can begin with 3-5 minutes and over time build up to 15 minutes or more. I know dedicated meditators who practice for 30 minutes every day. I hope one day I can grow up to be like them!

Hot Towel Scrub

Standing naked, fill the sink with hot water and add a few drops of essential oils. Try to find oils that are 100% pure without additives. They are the safest for your skin. I love lavender for the evening as it is relaxing. But you may try another oil such as grapefruit for invigorating or lemon for lifting the mood. Next, take a wash cloth and proceed to scrub your body quite vigorously with the oil and water from your neck on down to your toes. It should not be painful, but you may turn a lovely shade of pink in the process! At the end of the scrub, you will have released toxins, increased your circulation and given your body some positive, loving attention.

Part of the process of the hot towel scrub is to love your body just as it is, flaws and all. How comfortable are you with your body—stretch marks, wrinkles, extra weight, the whole nine yards? Are you ok standing naked and looking at yourself? For many, this may not be your idea of fun. When we are naked, we tend to feel vulnerable. We also criticize our bodies and wish it was more like this or more like that. Part of the emotional practice of the hot towel scrub is to accept your body with all its imperfections. None of us are perfect; that is what makes us unique. Learning to love your body as it is today is part of your self-care practice and giving yourself love and respect.

Massage & Touch

Whether we are shaking hands when we meet, hugging as we say goodbye or kissing our loved ones, humans need touch. We thrive on touch to connect with others and ourselves and learn about our feelings. Massage is one example of the wonderful ways we can release anxiety, stress and feel the loving kindness from one person to another. Massage and touch will reduce your cortisol, the stress hormone, and increase endorphins, the feel good hormone. You don't have to pay a professional massage therapist to receive such great care, although you can never beat an hour massage at the spa! You and your spouse can practice on each other. If your spouse is deployed, you will be missing your physical connection. Consider getting a monthly massage to help. It will raise your endorphins levels—they are your feel good hormone—and that will contribute to lowering your stress levels. Try using 100% essential oils with a carrier oil such as fractionated coconut oil and incorporating them into your massage. Communicate with each other. Tell your partner what you like, and ask them what and how they would like to be touched. It could be a simple foot massage while you are watching television or a head massage to ease the tension at the end of the day. Make sure you are hugging, kissing and touching each other daily. You may take a bath or shower together, cuddle together before going to sleep, or hold hands while out walking. No matter how small the gesture, it will not go unnoticed and it will pay off in the bigger picture of your relationship together. Touch does not always have to be sexual. I am only bringing to your attention the importance of physical touch and encouraging you and your spouse to be connected both physically and emotionally. Often couples lose this particular closeness in their lives that once brought them together; this can lead to loss of communication in other areas of their lives.

    In my coaching experience, I find that the longer a couple has been together, the more effort is needed to focus on the importance of continuing to build this bond. It is work to keep a physical relationship alive, but it's worth it. Sometimes one partner is more open to touch than another. Keep reaching out and making an effort. Make it one of your relationship priorities. Connecting physically for some may be easier than expressing your feelings verbally.

Earlier in the book, we talked about asking for what you want and getting what you need. Don't overlook that in regarding touch. What can you change today surrounding this part of your relationship with your spouse? How would you like it to look, what needs to happen to make a difference? If approaching this area of your relationship seems intimidating, offer this up to your spouse. They may feel the same way, and together you can come up with ways to ease into the comfort of touching each other and enjoying the connection. If needed you may seek professional help if you believe this area of your relationship needs a third party intervention.

Mindful Living and Spirituality

There is so much talk about mindful living, we sometimes think of mindful people as green, organic, hippy trip types! But in reality, we all have the innate ability to live a conscious life if we practice. So what does mindful living mean and how do you live a mindful life? I'd like to explore this area with you and help you find a place where you fit in. We are so used to living in a society that encourages us to be multi-dimensional beings. We are always multitasking, for example, when we're on the phone with a work call while checking our email inbox. Or we're cooking dinner for our kids at the same time as helping our high schooler do their math homework; we rarely allow ourselves to do one thing at a time. But this is our choice; we decide to run our lives on overload, and in turn we are not usually mindful of the moment. We hold the key to living a mindful life if we choose to take this direction. It does not come naturally to most of us, but we can all be successful in achieving conscious awareness if we are open to it.

Start with the simple act of taking a shower. Take a moment to think how this daily routine takes place for you. My guess is you are rushing. Do you dive in the shower, blast the water on your body, and attempt to shave your legs, underarms or face at the same time as washing your hair? Did you take the time to feel the warm or cool water on your body? How did the pressure of the water feel as it came down on your head? Did you smell the lovely organic shower gel that you took the time to pick out? This may all sound far too touchy feely for you, but hang with me a while here. Here's another example. When you're eating, what else are you doing at the same time? Surfing the web, playing on your phone? If so, stop and just take the time to eat, be in the moment. Smell and taste each bite and experience the texture of food and chew thoroughly. Enjoy the pure pleasure of eating. Train your mind to focus on the present. I ban all electronics from our dinner table! Meal times shouldn't be a time to make up time by multitasking. It should be a time to savor the food thoughtfully prepared for you or by you and to connect with family and friends. The additional plus to mindful eating is the ability to hone in on your appetite and recognize when you are full. Even meal preparation can be turned into a mindful moment practice. Next time you cook, light a candle, maybe enjoy a glass of wine, put on some relaxing music and enjoy thinking about what you are doing. Enjoy the process. You are providing the people you love with healthy, nutritious food. Some people find cooking a great time to chill out.

Mindful walking…this is similar to meditation walking with the exception that you are walking at your normal speed. Are you walking in your neighborhood or thinking about what you have to do tomorrow? I was talking with a neighbor recently about some of the wildlife, plants, and flowers in the neighborhood. She said, "Wow, I've never seen any of that. Where are you walking?!" I was walking the same place she was; the only difference is I was purposefully paying attention. I was training my mind to be in the moment. Are you observing your surroundings? Sure, you may have walked the dog around the same block a million times or more, but if you choose, you too will discover something new. Look around you, scan the sky, the plants, trees, homes, or whatever it is you see on your walk. Look at your surroundings with an open mind and curiosity like someone who landed on this planet for the first time!

Mindfulness in the bedroom…this is another area of concern that pops up for many spouses. Clients often share with me their frustration in their ability to transition from being the carer, the mother, father, teacher, the office commuter or something else to being the sexual lover they so want to be. They find it challenging being in touch with their body, their partner's body and the intimate connection they wish to create. This is very common. Don't worry, this can and will change the more you practice mindful living in all areas of your life. We have talked about touch, connection, and sexuality earlier; take a moment to think how you can be even more present when you and your partner make love. Where is your mind? On your grocery list, or thoughts of kids or the day's events? If so, try to find time to be alone before sex so you can center your mind and think about your partner and the amazing love that you share with each other. Do you have a difficult time switching from one behavior to another? What I mean by this is how easily can you turn off the monkey mind and be present. The more you practice mindful living in other areas of your life, the easier you will be able to relax and stay present in the bedroom. This will heighten your sexual experience and connection. Now that's mindful living worth the time and effort, right!

    Another time to focus on being mindful is when you spend time with family and friends. I don't know about you, but I find it a little bothersome when I am in a conversation with someone and they are either looking at their phone because it buzzed or scanning their Apple watch because it gave them a poke! I understand we all have commitments and things we need to keep track of, but how did we manage back in the day before technology took over our pace of life? How difficult is it to let all the pings and dings of social media subside for an hour while we just talk and be present for those we care about? Can you imagine in my coaching practice if I put my attention on electronic devices when I was working with a client? I'd be out of a job! Look into the person's face that you are talking with, really listen to them, and be cognizant of the conversation taking place. Practice placing time limits on your electronic devices, not just when you are with others but also when you are alone. Don't get me wrong, I'm not ready to live in a commune and give up on technology, but it can be a time waster and in some cases an emotional energy drainer.

So where does spirituality fit into living a mindful life? More often than not, people associate spirituality with religion. Naturally, they can go together, but they don't have to. An individual may be extremely spiritual but have no religious following. Where are you in this sphere of your world? What I have experienced when coaching clients is those people who have a strong spirituality to the bigger picture around them, whatever that means to them, are happier people. If you find worshiping a particular religion brings you peace and clarity, be sure to make time in your life to commit to this. That may be something as simple as reading passages from the Bible in the evenings, attending a Bible study group or being part of your parish services.

On the other hand, if you do not have a religious connection, it is important to find what speaks to you and helps you get closer to your center. The place where peace can be found. Nature is one of those places that will join your heart and soul to a place that can be bathed in tranquility, allowing you to escape the demands of life. The simple things in life that we so often take for granted and overlook are where our answers lie in our vision of creating a mindful life for ourselves.

"I go to Nature to be soothed and healed; to have my senses put in tune once more."
John Burroughs

Journaling

I started journaling many years ago. To build a journaling habit requires commitment. As you begin to regularly write in your journal, you will see how this simple practice will start to impact your life. When we journal, we are emphasizing the *4 Cornerstones Of Life: Acceptance, Flexibility, Change And Empathy*. Journaling will draw upon all these areas and help us to give gratitude for the lives we lead. Every morning I sit in my meditation nook, which is a space in my home.

At present it happens to be an alcove under the stairs, but as you can guess the location changes with every move! In this space I purchased a bench from Ikea that fits snuggly in the small space. Imagine you are in a sleeping berth on a small sail boat. I told you it was a small area—not much head room! I placed some of my favorite cushions on the bench, a lavender scented candle sits on the floor, and there's also a basket of inspirational books that I read from here and there. One of my favorites is a book by Bernie Siegel, titled *365 Prescriptions for the Soul*. I have some artwork on the wall, small prints from England. I made my meditation nook inviting.

Most mornings before the kids wake up you will find me on my bench writing and drinking a mug of

English breakfast tea! I recommend journaling to all my clients. At first, some people see an empty canvas and shrink, not knowing what to write. Here are some steps to get the ball rolling:

- Purchase a beautiful journal, one that appeals to you, and some pens, pencils, and markers, etc.
- Identify a space in your home that brings you tranquility and beckons you to sit for a while. Go to this space every time you journal. Choosing the same place when you write will help solidify the writing habit.
- Pick a time - choose a time that you know you can stick to. For me, early mornings before the kids get up is a guaranteed time that I can write without being disturbed. Journaling doesn't work in-between packing school lunches or answering work emails. You need focus. Writing at the same time daily will help to make your habit stick.
- Write down ten things you are thankful for either from the day before or that day. These do not have to be profound, life-changing thoughts, just simple memories of things that brought you joy and gratitude.

Here is my list for today:

- My health
- My family
- Hearing my daughter laugh with her friend
- The rain cooling down the heat of the day
- Finding a parking space with ease!
- Glass of wine with my husband
- The beautiful white orchid plant I just bought
- Seeing a big green and orange lizard climbing a tree
- Seeing a bright yellow tiny bird - not sure what kind it was?
- Getting my workout done earlier than usual

You may be wondering how keeping a gratitude journal can impact your life. Writing down things we are thankful for connects us to our life in a meaningful way. It brings awareness and helps us to take notice of the small things we already have in our lives and to learn how to appreciate them more. These little tokens of mindfulness encourage us to be present and not always searching for a big event to make us happy.

Let's Purge!

The second part I add to my gratitude journal is to write down anything that comes to my mind. This act of purging, if you like, helps to clear your thoughts and make way for a more positive day ahead. You can rant and rave, write about your sorrows or something that makes you happy. You can write about where you are in life and why you may have a certain feeling that you have. There is no right or wrong thing to put in your journal. Some days I find myself waffling on for 30 minutes, and other days I have little to say. I love those short days; I feel I must be more in tune with my reality and at peace when nothing bleeds from my soul on to the paper. Remember, no one is going to read this but you. No need to hide your journal under your mattress like you did when you were a teenager!

A Senses Journal

I have some clients who feel stuck when asked to write down ten things they appreciate. So one day I suggested to a client that she try for five things, and then I got to thinking about our five senses. So along came the concept of the senses journal. To begin a senses journal, you think about taste, smell, sight, sound, and touch. You write one thing for each sense that you have been blessed with that day. Try this simple writing activity. Here is mine from today:

- Taste - the steaming hot cup of green tea I drank this afternoon
- Smell - of my Indian tikka curry I had for lunch!
- Sight - my kids' smiling faces
- Sound - my husband playing the piano
- Touch - the cool, smooth clay when I was working on my ceramics

Is there something else you'd like to generate in your journal?

Some people enjoy writing poetry. They just feel a poem come to them, and away they go. This has happened to me a couple of times, which is surprising as I am not a poet! Other clients tell me they like to doodle with colored markers, and others who are more artistic might sketch a scene from their imagination or a landscape they see. Whatever helps you to bring a sense of gratefulness and calm to your day is a good thing. Journaling in any way you choose can only add value to your life. So go ahead, let your mind wander, relax, write and maybe even draw!

    The other benefit from journaling is the reflection. You can re-read over past entries and ponder on your words. It is a way to clarify thoughts and get a deeper understanding into why you are feeling a certain way and how you may resolve a situation. Reflection is an important part of emotional growth. Reading past journal entries may inspire you to tackle a new challenge. You may find you are better equipped to work out the lay of the land because you were able to reflect on a similar situation and how you dealt with it.

Exercise 16 – Mindful Living Action Steps

Look at your Inner Peace mind map and take note of one or two areas that relate to mindful living. Plan your next steps in how you are going to achieve those desires. What can you do today that will get you one step closer to achieving a more mindful life? For example, you may be hoping to practice meditation. Choose a time of day, possibly set a reminder on your phone as an alert, and begin to carve out time in your day to make it happen. Or maybe you live next to a beautiful park or another scenic spot, but you rarely visit it. Schedule a time each week to do just that. If you want to live a mindful life, you need to take action steps to create one.

On the Road Again…

As a military spouse, you are no stranger to moving. Some of you will have moved more times than you can count on two hands. I know I'm getting up there in the double digits. Moving house is said to be one of the most stressful things that you can do in life. It's right up there with losing a loved one and divorce. It has been said that high-stress situations such as this can even shorten your life. I hope not or else I may only have a decade left to live! All jokes aside, let's talk about how to ease the stress of moving. I would say almost every military spouse that I work with will ask me how to keep moving and dealing with the emotional stresses that go with it. I could offer up a whole bunch of how to tips for organizing your kid's closet of toys, right down to where to put those pesky sticky notes that sometimes the packers fail to see, only to find on the other end of the move your kitchen dishes are in the master bedroom, and your toiletries are in the garage and why did they pack a burnt out light bulb? I could even go as far as telling you not to worry, it'll all work itself out. But you've heard all this before.

 I'd like you to identify what is worrying you most about your move beyond the physical packing up part, which sure does get old after a while but is unavoidable. Look a little deeper. What is making you anxious? Is it moving to a place you do not know anyone, leaving behind your work, the thought of your children having to start a new school and the anxiety that they may experience?

Exercise 17 - Face Your Fears

Once you have identified your biggest fears, you are going to face them head on, conquer them and thrive with your moves. Here's how.

First journal your concerns. When you have written down your thoughts and worries, notice how those troubles are now on paper and in a place to be rationalized. For example, you may have written that leaving your friend behind is sad. Flip the switch and write down all the great memories you have had with that person and how lucky you are to have such a wonderful friendship. Before you leave them, plan a set time each week or month to talk. Look forward to sharing your new experiences with them when you settle into your new hometown.

Another example may be just the sheer physical fatigue that comes with yet again having to unpack another box and build another home. Consider a full unpack of your household goods. This is part of the moving company's service. I think it's awesome, but it's not for everyone. The packers do not put away your items; they will lay them in any open place in your home. But it sure saves on dealing with the flattening out of paper and boxes—that's my nemesis! Turn this pessimistic attitude of your move into a positive one and see your next home as an opportunity to decorate in a new way, perhaps adding a different twist than usual. Look at this move as an opportunity to reconfigure your furniture into new places. Get creative and have fun with it. You could also use this time to declutter and donate any unwanted household goods, clothes, books or toys, etc. Decluttering is so refreshing and energizing.

Maybe you identified job searching as your frustration along with your irritation of leaving your current job yet again. Use this opportunity to explore new options within your field or outside of it. It is also an opportunity to make new friendships at work and get excited about the new work environment and the challenge associated with that. Whatever is worrying you, write it down. The next step is to use your journal pages and come up with some plausible reasons that counteract the negative thoughts. Whatever it is that is eating you up, turning your thoughts around and counteracting those voices of doubt with optimism will help. Revisit the *4 Cornerstones Of Life, Empathy, Change, Flexibility And Acceptance* held together with gratitude, and as you encounter negative voices in your head about your upcoming move, use the *4 Cornerstones* to help you rationalize your thoughts and embrace the change.

At the end of the day, if you want to be with your spouse and live a military life with more ease and grace, you have to accept change, and moving is part of the deal. I discovered the sooner I accepted this, even though it comes with some turmoil, the easier my life became. Use your moves as a time of reflection, not rejection. In your journal write down what you did not do at your current duty station that you look forward to trying out when you move. What is unique to where you are moving to that you are looking forward to learning more about? How will this move impact the bigger picture of your spouse's career and your family's future? What can you identify with as something you'll look forward to doing in your next home? When you do this, you will turn your move into a positive life experience and an opportunity for personal growth.

Only you can make this thought process happen. If you continue to work on your mind maps and find out what you want from each move and where you want your life to take you and how you are going to make that happen, you will have some control over your life. For many of us, I feel that is the missing link. We need to feel we have choices and independence. By laying the foundations of what you want with each new location you call home, you are making your life choices. You are creating a purpose driven life. Consider all the wonderful opportunities you have had with every place you have lived. Think about how they have sculpted you and how you have grown and learned something new about yourself with each one of those moves. Without those moves, you would not have experienced this personal growth or exciting adventures and new experiences.

You are the only one who has the power to create a full life. No one can do this for you, and it's not easy to keep rebuilding your life. It takes physical and emotional stamina. This is a rather bold and blunt statement to make, but let's face it—what's the alternative? The move is going to happen; the sooner we get on board and create something to look forward to, the better for both our emotional and physical health. By having a great attitude, you will help yourself and everyone around you. If you fight the given situation, you will hurt yourself and in turn those you love. Don't get me wrong; I understand this is no easy task I am asking of you. Your spouse is not trying to punish you or hurt you by asking you to move yet again. This is the life we are learning to thrive in, not just survive in. *Flexibility, acceptance, change and empathy,* your new friends the *4 Cornerstones of Life*, are your key to a future of greater ease. They are the only way to move forward and continue to bring gratitude into your life.

Once you begin to make mindful living and spirituality a part of your life by putting into practice acts of self-care and mindfulness, you will notice other things in your life are easier to address. Be present, look at the moon, see the morning sunrise, stop and smell the flowers, watch the rain fall down your window pane, enjoy a quiet cup of tea as you listen to the thunder—you get my point, right? Bringing all your senses to the forefront of your mind every day will bring you a joyful life. You will roll with the punches a little easier. Everything seems just that bit brighter; you will find the *4 Cornerstones* we talked about in chapter one—*empathy, acceptance, flexibility, and change*—are evident in your daily life. Together those *4 Cornerstones* will keep you grounded along with *gratitude*, the glue of life. To succeed in your military life, you must keep a positive mindset. At times we have to recognize that the best thing we can do is surrender, control the controllable and leave the rest to the universe. Usually, those stars will align.

Just breathe.

Chapter 6

Vitality

When you think of the word vitality, what picture do you create in your mind? Does this image mesh with how you feel? Having vim and vigor is essential and possible no matter what age you are. As a military spouse it is essential that you have great health and a huge amount of energy to see you through the months and years that come and go so you can live your military life with ease. Some of the information presented in this chapter is unique to you and your military life. You may be someone who is lucky enough to have energy and zest. On the other hand, you may be wondering how you get to feel that way. Whichever spectrum of the scale you are on, I can help you by offering some suggestions you can try to feel vibrant, healthy, sexy and full of pizzazz! It all begins with what is on the end of your fork. Could it be that simple? Yes, it could! The fork to the bedroom and everything in between is what we will scrutinize! Vitality not only comes from the food we eat but also the quality of our sleep and the exercise we engage in. For you, this means bringing to light an ideal and manageable way of living. It will be your personal vitality roadmap.

I'll start on Monday…!

Have you ever said these words only to find that another Monday has come and gone and you made no change to your eating patterns? If so, you have become a victim of the diet industry. The diet industry is easily a multimillion dollar money making scheme. It is out there playing on the emotions of millions of people every day. We are bombarded with photo shopped images of men and women striking a sexy pose with an airbrushed healthy glow, usually under a misleading and often unreasonable caption convincing us that 'this is the diet you won't want to miss.' We are led to believe that 'this is the one great fix that will solve all our problems.' Diets don't work. PLEASE don't diet anymore! Yes, I said no more diets. I need you to get off that CRAZY train! This is why.

The problem with diets is that over an extended period of dieting and extreme calorie restriction our bodies go into protection mode. Our bodies are protecting us from starving to death. If we do not consume enough calories or we have lost a lot of weight by eating very few calories, our bodies switch into 'starvation mode.' Our bodies are designed this way so that our ancestors way back could survive if they did not come home from a hunt with food to eat. Restricting calories and some possible food groups slows down our metabolism. This means you may now have to eat fewer calories than you did before losing weight just to prevent you from gaining back the weight you initially lost. Along with metabolism changes come hormonal changes. The hormone leptin that is responsible for alerting us on when we feel full and satisfied is not as reliable. Food that once left you feeling satiated does not do the job anymore, and now you feel hungrier than you did when you were on a diet. Even neurological changes take place when people are dieting. People begin to display obsessive behaviors about food. Have you ever had a day where you are always thinking about food so much that those thoughts leave you searching for food all day long? That was OK when we were hunters and gathers, but it's not so helpful when we are surrounded by food in the office or at home. Are the donuts and bagels calling your name again?

It is human nature to want to start and finish a diet within a given time frame. We all want to feel successful. But if, for example, you go on a detox diet, say, for five days and lose 5-10lbs, once you resume your regular eating habits, you will gain back what you lost and possibly a little more. Anytime you greatly restrict your food intake, it can backfire, and the weight you lost may come back to haunt you.

Unfortunately, the answer is not to order that supersize meal and fill up on pastries. I need you to start being an intuitive eater. Mindful eating is about thinking about what you are eating, how the foods you eat make you feel and paying attention to when you are comfortably full and stopping eating when you get there. It is also about fueling your body with nutritious and energizing foods that'll sustain you and make you feel great. No foods are off limits. After all, food is pleasurable and we want to enjoy our favorite foods and live a great life, right? So, if you crave chocolate or fries you can have them guilt free but in moderation. Moderation is essential to your success. Building this kind of relationship with food is building a balanced body and one which is on the road to steady weight loss. Eating nutritious foods in the appropriate serving size and cutting back on unhealthy processed foods will be your weight loss weapon. Weight loss ideally should come off at a steady pace. Some people lose weight quickly in the beginning and then slow down later on. That is OK. You should aim for 1/4lb - 1lb per week for weight loss.

WOW, imagine your life, eating what you like without obsessing over calories, fats, carbs and "bad" foods. How does it look? Don't panic, people! For some, the thought of eating forbidden food strikes up images of their bodies ballooning. But if you eat mindfully, you can achieve a healthy, maintainable weight. Maintainable means a weight that is not difficult to sustain, a place where your body has reached homeostasis. We all have that place, and we can get there without stressing our bodies both physically and emotionally with diets that don't work. Part of my work in coaching clients is to discover a way of eating that works for them and their family. Life is complicated enough; what you eat shouldn't be. Not only do we look at the physical how to of meal planning and such, but we also take a more in depth look at their unique food needs. We analyze what they are eating and how food is making them feel both physically and emotionally. So often I find that people do not understand the connection between food and their emotional health. What we eat impacts every area of our lives. Let's begin with the basics. I want you to leave the images of all those food pyramids and the government's USDA food plates behind. We are on the journey to creating your nutritional road map. This will take a little time, patience and a willingness to be open to change and trying new foods. Are you ready? Awesome, let's go!

Whole Foods

The simplest way to explain this is to examine wholes foods in their natural state at the time of harvesting. When a farmer yields his crops, he collects all the vegetables, fruits, sugar cane and grains such as wheat, corn, barley, millet or whatever he is growing and plucks it from the earth in its purest, healthiest form. What you see is what you get—a carrot that looks and tastes like a carrot, wheat that looks like wheat, potatoes with skin on it and dirt! You get it! From there the food gets shipped to the four corners of the globe, and this is when it starts to look ugly and problems develop. Some of this beautiful, natural food is sent on to processing factories where it is stripped of all its goodness and changed into another form of the original food. For example, whole grains are stripped of their bran and germ and made into refined grains. They are robbed of their dietary fiber and some of their iron and B vitamins. Processing foods extend their shelf life, but it doesn't necessarily extend ours! Corn is turned inside out during processing and made into corn syrup, corn flour, and other corn derivatives. Vegetables and fruits get canned and coated in sugar, artificial flavors and preservatives, and on and on it goes. What once resembled food has now been changed and taken on a new identity.

Food today is not like it was years back. There are so many convenience foods, and it comes in all kinds of shapes and forms. We have cheese in tubes, hamburger meat in a cardboard box, cereal the color of crayons in your kid's crayon box, and vegetables in cans that could outlive a nuclear attack! Then we are bombarded by fads such as fat-free, sugar-free, low fat and high fat. It's insane what we put into our bodies kidding ourselves that is it wholesome. Processed foods are taking over people's pantries. Anything that comes in a can or a box has been processed in some way. Do I rely on some foods that come from a package? Of course I do! However, I always look for the cleanest item I can find. Clean means they are always free from food dyes and preservatives, they have a high-fiber, low-sugar content, and they tend to be organic when I can get them. I will also add that these packaged foods are not a staple in my family's daily diet. The typical packaged foods my family eats are foods such as whole grain cereal, blue corn chips, the occasional jar of salsa if I am not in the mood to make my own that week, whole grain bread and crackers, and some sweet treats such as a little candy or chocolate.

As a nation, we have allowed ourselves to lead such fast-paced and frenzied lives that we have lost touch with reality. How often do you sit together in your house and have a family dinner, one that is also home cooked? We are so rushed we cannot even find the time to dedicate 20-30 minutes to cook dinner and 15-20 minutes to eat together. That's a total of a little over 60 minutes out of a 24 hour period. What's wrong with this picture? We believe we have no time; we have trapped ourselves to become dependent on packaged and frozen ready-made meals. If we make something 'from scratch' we are in awe of that person who took on the feat! But is it that impressive of a feat to eat pure, clean whole foods? No! It can be easy if not faster than driving to the store, wandering down the food aisle looking at frozen dinners and coming home with a frozen chicken dinner that barely resembles chicken or real potatoes and vegetables. If you eat processed foods, your health will be affected negatively. It's that simple.

Have you considered how many people today live with illnesses such as type 2 diabetes, thyroid disease, obesity, heart disease, hypertension, liver disease, attention deficit disorder, attention deficit hyperactivity disorder or disorders of the digestive tract? I'm not a doctor, but I honestly believe that many of these illnesses could be prevented or even reversed by eating clean. If people do not change the way their families eat, we will have a massive health crisis on our hands by the time our children are our age. We already spend billions of dollars a year treating such diseases. Despite all of these sicknesses, people will argue that we live longer today than ever before. This is a true statement, but how enjoyable is your life when you are sick, tired and hurting both physically and emotionally and your breakfast not only consists of a bowl of cornflakes but also a handful of medications to help you live? Is that a life worth living? Could it be different? We need to take action and put our priority on preventative health care. Of course, I do believe there is a place for medications, and without a doctor's intervention, some people would be very sick and possibly die. However, when we talk about how to live a vital life, we need to begin with clean eating. To ensure your best health, your "medicine" is on the end of your fork.

This quote from the Dalai Lama is such a perfect example of where the nation's physical and emotional health is at today. When he was asked what surprised him about humanity he said:

> *"Man. Because he sacrifices his health in order to make money. Then he sacrifices money to recuperate his health. And then he is so anxious about the future that he does not enjoy the present; the result being that he does not live in the present or the future; he lives as if he is never going to die, and then dies having never really lived."*

Read the quote again. How does it sit with you? As a military spouse, can you relate to it? The military lifestyle is a long and sometimes arduous journey. Without a good lifestyle and work balance, how are you holding down your fort? Are your foundations there but they sometimes come under attack by too many commitments? Can you learn to prioritize some of your commitments better and learn to let some things slide? *Holding Down The Fort* does not just apply to your family and home; it also relates to your body, your physical and emotional health. You have to live in your body for a long time to come. If you don't take care of your fort, where are you going to live? When your spouse retires from the military, I want you to both be able to reap the rewards of all your hard work.

Exercise 18 - Pantry and Freezer Overhaul

I see you cringing! "Oh no!" I hear you say. Fear not, you won't regret this little exercise. By completing this task, you will be one step closer to achieving vitality.

Take an afternoon to overhaul your pantry and freezer. Clear off a surface in your kitchen that you can lay out all your processed foods. I will allow you to keep some of them, so don't despair, providing they fit into the following criteria:

- Fiber: 3 grams or more per serving
- Sugar: less than 9 grams per serving—I'm being generous here too!
- Free from artificial dyes
- Free from preservatives: a good rule of thumb here is if you don't know what it is and you cannot pronounce it, it shouldn't be in your body! This is what I teach my kids.

Whatever food is off limits, consider donating it to a food bank. I know it is not the healthiest donation, but it is better than the alternative of throwing it in the garbage can and wasting money. The food bank will be thankful.

Now, look at what is left. You should be left with primarily whole foods. They are your proteins, carbohydrates, fats and fresh produce. We will now examine each of these areas.

Carbohydrates and Their Bad Rap!

Carbohydrates fall into two categories, complex carbohydrates and simple carbohydrates. Complex are the 100% whole grains such as wheat, barley, millet, kamut, kashi, bulgur, spelt, amaranth, quinoa, oats, brown and wild rice, lentils, beans, and corn. They can also be found in fresh fruits and many vegetables, including root vegetables such as carrots, parsnips and squashes such as butternut, acorn, pumpkin squash, yams, sweet potatoes, and peas.

Why do we hear of so many people avoiding carbohydrates like they are the devil? There are so many variations on diets out there that are either low or carbohydrate free. It is no wonder people are lost on what to do for the best. People have demonized all carbohydrates, which is a shame as complex carbohydrates can be an excellent food source.

There is no need to avoid eating complex carbohydrates as long as your body has no problems digesting them and you do not have a health challenge that requires you to limit your carbohydrate intake such as PCOS - poly cystic ovary syndrome, Type 1 or 2 diabetes or someone who eats lots of carbs (more than 250 g per day) or if you are unable to lose weight.

The media has led us to believe that all carbohydrates lead to weight gain and a higher body fat percentage. Naturally, if your portion sizes are too large, they will make you gain weight, but so will most foods if eaten with gusto, compounded with not getting enough exercise. By controlling your portion size, eating complex carbs should be a part of your diet. Complex carbohydrates are the place where you can get lots of fiber, which will help you to feel full for longer and have a smooth operating digestive tract. They are an excellent source of minerals and vitamins, including all of your B vitamins such as Thiamin, riboflavin, niacin, folic acid, pyridoxine, biotin and cyanocobalamin, which is B12. They act as your primary fuel source in your body which both your brain and your body need to function. When we eat a complex carbohydrate, they digest slowly and turn into glucose. Because of this, they do not raise your blood sugar as quickly, like simple carbohydrates tend to do. The right amount of glucose is necessary for thyroid function. But if you take in too many carbs your body will produce too much glucose and then put you at risk for insulin resistance. How much is too much depends on each person. Hence, this is one of the many reasons why we cannot look at nutrition with a cookie cutter approach.

Carbs are also helpful in balancing your hormones. People with thyroid issues, adrenal fatigue, hypoglycemia folks, endurance athletes and those trying to conceive or are postpartum and breast feeding should be consuming some complex carbohydrates.

Your thyroid hormone T4, which is the inactive hormone the thyroid needs to convert itself into the active form, which is T3, so that your body can function as it's designed to do. T3 is your vitality juice, your vim and vigor. Without that conversion, you will feel drained, cranky, have trouble losing weight or possibly continue to gain weight. Women are more susceptible to thyroid dysfunction than men, especially women who are in their fertile prime years, peri menopausal or in menopause. If you are consuming less than 50 grams of carbs per day, you could be putting your body at risk of needing thyroid medication. Thyroid medication helps your liver to convert T4.

If you are someone who has been diagnosed with adrenal fatigue, you need complex carbohydrates to support adrenal function. Your adrenal glands help the production of other hormones your body makes. Going on a low carb diet in this situation may hinder the healing of your adrenals.

Scan your body; how is your energy level? Have you ever felt weak, lethargic and moody? Maybe you are not taking in enough complex carbs. Take some time to look at what type of carbohydrates you are eating, how much and how often.

Our bodies all have unique needs; this is not a one size fits all approach. When I work with clients, we discover the best fit for their body. Some people require more carbs than others.

Then there is the question of organic versus conventional. If you can afford to buy organic, this is your best option. This way you can avoid adding unwanted chemicals into your body. But if going 100% organic is not an option, perhaps picking and choosing the grains you eat more of and making those organic could be a good option for you and your family. Also, try buying in bulk or wholesale for a more cost-effective option. I sure wish I could have a 100% organic diet, but dependent on where I live that is not always an option. So I will pick and choose what and when I buy organic.

Simple carbohydrates are those found in food items made with refined white flour and sugar, usually cookies, white rice, cakes, cereal, white bread, crackers, pretzels, chips, doughnuts, soda, and candy. They are incredibly addictive and not at all good for your health or longevity, even the organic options!

When you eat simple carbs, they digest fairly quickly in your system and raise your blood sugar rapidly. The excess sugar in your body that cannot be used will increase your body fat percentage and up the number on the scale. Have you ever had a slice of cake and a sweetened latte only to find an hour later you are tired out? Simple carbs will do this to you; they leave you feeling tired and listless and even hypoglycemic. If you know you are addicted to simple carbs, I suggest you wean yourself off them and replace them with wholesome complex carbs.

Weaning yourself off these types of simple carbs takes time and patience. You will have days that you crave sugar, possibly experience headaches and feel tired. Stick with it; your body is trying to normalize its blood sugar levels. The good news is once you switch from simple to complex carbs you will feel like a new person! You will have lots more energy, and your mood will be more stable. Begin by switching to 100% whole grains with your meals, trading white flour for 100%whole wheat flour when you bake or a minimum of half and half. Try alternatives to white table sugar such as coconut sugar, raw honey and 100% maple syrup. Keep in mind that even though you are consuming a healthier option, overeating will lead to weight gain.

I am not saying that you can never again enjoy a slice of chocolate cake or your favorite pasta dish or enjoy some delicious sourdough bread! Savor all of those things, but eat healthy alternatives the rest of the time. When you look at your diet, 80-85% of the time should be clean eating all the way, and the other 10-15% is left for those treats you love. Treats are okay here and there, but should not be part of your daily diet.

What is a Protein?

There are different options for adding protein into your diet. There are animal proteins and plant based proteins. Clients will ask which is the best type to eat and how much they should consume. This is all dependent upon what works best for your body.

We all have different DNA that is made up of cells and blood that feed muscles and bones and nourish our organs. Protein's job in the body is to support these systems. If you do not get enough protein in your diet, your tissues and cells will not be able to function. Each protein molecule is made up of amino acids. Our body can make some of these amino acids on its own. These are nonessential amino acids. But the others we need to get from our daily diet as our body has no way to store this macronutrient. The amino acids we get from food are often referred to as essential amino acids. Without getting too scientific, think of amino acids as the building blocks for healthy muscles, tissues, and organs. They build muscles and repair them, protect your immune system, help to balance hormones, and can be used as an energy source if needed. This would be the case if your body had no carbohydrates to use for energy. Replacing essential amino acids with high-quality protein is important.

Animal proteins are also known as complete proteins. This means they provide you with all the essential amino acids. They are foods that come from an animal: meat, dairy, eggs, and seafood. Some are leaner than others, so fish and chicken are a lighter cleaner protein option in comparison to red meat.

Plant proteins are whole grains, lentils, beans, soy, nuts, and seeds. These are incomplete proteins. If you are a vegetarian or a vegan, you will need to ensure that you take in a wide variety of all of these types of proteins daily so that you can provide your body with all the essential amino acids. This is because not all plant based proteins have all the essential amino acids.

How much should you take in? To maintain healthy bodily function, the Recommended Daily Allowance (RDA) for protein is 0.4-0.5 grams per pound (0.8–1.0g/kg) of body weight for a healthy adult per day. But if you have a specific goal in mind, for example, if you are trying to put on more muscle mass, your body may need more than suggested. Some people do well on the minimum amount of protein, whereas others need more. This is why it is so important to not only pay attention to what you are eating but how the food you eat is making you feel.

Not All Proteins Are Created Equally

Look at the options available to you. Let's begin by looking at red meat, using beef as an example. There are organic red meats, which mean cows that are roaming free, chomping on grass and living a beautiful, happy life—just the way cows should live! So if animal welfare is a concern to you, this will be an important factor to consider when purchasing beef. Additionally, these cows are fed a diet of grass and/or grains that have not been sprayed with pesticides. Organic also ensures they have not been given any hormones or antibiotics. Next, we have grass fed beef. These cows have been fed only grass, hay, and forage. They live their lives in the open and are not penned in like conventional cattle. But it does mean that they could have been exposed to pesticides and hormones. Last is conventional beef—cheaper yes, but not good for your health. Conventional beef is exposed to pesticides, antibiotics, and hormones. The cows are fed cheap food sources and confined to small living spaces where they are open to disease, hence the need for routine antibiotics.

If you can afford organic or grass fed red meat instead of the conventional red meat, go for it. Grass fed and organically grown is more expensive, but the benefits to your health are a plus. You will avoid exposing your body to harmful pollutants such as chemicals, hormones, and antibiotics. One of the advantages of grass fed meats is their high omega 3 fats, which are the good fats that help with heart health and hormonal balance. Some people find grass fed meat easier to digest than conventional red meat. I agree it is hard to get your head around sometimes paying double or more for organic and grass fed meats, but I look at it as health insurance. I am committing to fueling my body and my family's bodies with healthier options that will enable us to be healthier and avoid the doctor's office. Another way to make red meat more doable on the family budget is to limit the number of times you eat red meat each week. If you are only eating red meat occasionally, it may be financially doable. This is a very good time to explore vegetarian options and begin introducing some plant based meals into your family's weekly diet. Eating vegetarian meals tends to be very cost effective as grains, lentils and produce are cheaper than meat and seafood.

Leaner Options

Seafood, dairy, eggs and lean cuts of pork are some leaner options of protein. I would advise you to choose carefully. Here are some guidelines on choosing the cleanest options that will offer the best nutritional value.

Seafood is best if it is wild caught. They are higher in vitamin D, B12, B6, selenium, and magnesium. Some wild fish such as salmon have elevated levels of Omega 3 and 6 fatty acids, around 20% more than farm raised salmon. It is balanced just right so your body can use the fatty acids efficiently. When you eat wild caught fish, you can be assured you are staying clear of pesticides, antibiotics and other harmful chemicals. Wild caught fish has not been fed a filler type diet that often contains corn; this is common practice in farm raised fish. The one negative side effect to eating some fish is the mercury content. Mercury is higher in the following:

- Chilean sea bass
- Bluefish
- Halibut
- Sablefish (black cod)
- Spanish mackerel (Gulf)
- Fresh tuna (except skipjack)

Lower mercury options are:
- Salmon
- Tilapia
- Shrimp
- Tuna (canned-light)
- Cod
- Catfish

The other reason to limit your wild caught fish intake to no more than twice a week is that the oceans are being over-fished.

Other great options for lean protein are pasture raised pork, organic chicken and organic dairy and pastured eggs. Organic dairy is becoming more readily available at wholesale stores now, making it a more affordable option for more people. Dairy was the first organic food I switched my family to years ago. If you remember, earlier we were talking about the antibiotics and hormones in conventionally raised cattle. Consider this: whatever they eat or whatever is introduced into their bodies then goes into ours. Our bodies are becoming more resistant to antibiotics, and I believe one of the reasons for this is our food chain. We are consuming antibiotics through some food sources without even knowing it. Today my family and I eat minimal dairy, and if we do it is organic.

Organic eggs and chicken have a higher nutritional value than conventionally raised chicken. Organic chickens tend to be smaller than conventional. That is because they are not pumped full of growth hormones and fed a nasty diet of GMO feed. Organic eggs taste so much better than conventional, and they have a higher nutritional value. I know they can be pricey, but if you shop around you can find deals in wholesale markets and possibly your local farmers market. Search online for farms that will deliver food to your home.

Pork in the United States by law has to be antibiotic free. Pork tenderloin is one of the leanest cuts of meat from a pig. Problems from pork arise when it is changed into bacon, sausage, salami and deli meats such as ham. They are processed in a factory where nitrates are added. Nitrates help to preserve the meats and add color; this is harmful to our health. These preservatives and dyes can cause hypertension, migraines and some cancers. There are good alternative nitrate free pork products readily available at most grocery stores. Always be sure to read the ingredients list to know what you are purchasing.

Plants...Yum!

It is a very good idea to explore vegetarian cooking. It is a healthy, cheap alternative in comparison to other proteins, especially if you eat seasonally and locally. One of the obvious reasons people choose to be vegetarian is their personal feelings toward animal welfare and saving the planet by reducing the carbon footprint. Both of these hot topic items are worth considering. Even if you are a part time vegetarian like me, it all helps the planet and our health. Vegetarian meals do not consist of only vegetables! Get creative; you can incorporate complex carbohydrates such as high fiber grains, organic soy, beans, peas, lentils, nuts, fruits and seeds into the dishes you cook. There are many online recipe sites that can help you to get started—www.allrecipes.com is one of my go-to websites.

Some of the benefits of eating plant based meals are lower cholesterol, lower blood pressure, better blood sugar levels and weight loss. When you begin adding vegetarian meals into your diet, take note of how you feel. Do you feel fuller for longer, energized, tired? How does this compare to eating meat or seafood? Also, pay attention to how you feel the following day. What you eat will affect how you function for 24 hours or more. Begin eating plant based meals twice a week and gradually add in a third day or more if you find it agrees with your body.

Fats, the Good the Bad and the Ugly!

We need fat in our diets. There was a diet fad in the early 80's when everyone was eating fat-free everything—what a disaster! People didn't realize that the fat-free food had a higher sugar content, which in excess gets stored as fat. The type of fat we digest is important to understand. Below I will outline the different types of fat and what foods they are found in and how often you should eat them.

Saturated Fat

Saturated fats are solid at room temperature. They are the fats that are the culprits of raising a person's LDL levels, the "bad" fat in a cholesterol screening test. If you have a higher than desired ratio of this type of cholesterol in your blood, you are putting yourself at risk for heart disease. This is because LDL cholesterol is the type of molecule that sticks to your artery walls and causes a plaque build-up. Saturated fats are found in meats such as beef, poultry, and pork. It is also in milk and milk products, avocados, palm oil and coconut products such as coconut oil and milk. There are many differences of opinion when it comes to deciding how much saturated fat a person should consume. When I work with my clients, I base it upon their health history, health goals and how foods are making them feel. So without sounding too evasive, I cannot tell you what the perfect amount of saturated fat is for you personally. Assess your situation and base your decisions upon that. In the news recently there has been a lot of interest in coconut oil. It is unfortunate that the media are tainting coconut oil as the enemy. I beg to differ, and I know many others would agree with me. The same goes for avocados. They are an excellent source of healthy fat even though they fall under the umbrella of saturated fats.

Monounsaturated Fat

    This is a fat that is liquid at room temperature but is solid when chilled. They are great for raising your HDL (high-density lipoprotein), which is your good cholesterol, and lowering your LDL (low-density lipoprotein). They are found in olives, olive oil, seeds, nuts, avocados, and fish such as halibut and mackerel. They are all high in oleic acid. These fats are great for your heart, and you should consume them daily.

Polyunsaturated Fats

This type of fat is also known as omega 3 and 6 (EPA eicosapentaenoic acid and DHA docosahexaenoic acid). They are found in salmon, herring, trout, sardines, fresh tuna, flax seed and flax oil, walnuts and soy bean oil. They raise your good cholesterol and lower your bad. These fabulous fats help us reduce oxidative stress, promote memory and help to stabilize our moods. They play a significant role in reducing inflammation in your body. That's why we so often hear of people consuming fish oils if they have arthritis or other joint pain. If you decide that you would prefer to take your omega 3 and 6 in capsule form in addition to your diet, that is OK providing you read the labels carefully. When taking fish oil capsules, you need to find products that are tested for mercury. You do not want to take a supplement that contains mercury.

Trans Fatty Acid

You must avoid trans fat 100% of the time. When you read the label, it will say partially hydrogenated oils—this is a trans fat. You will find it in bread, candy, chips, cookies, pastries, margarine and some peanut butter. It is a processed fat created by adding hydrogen to liquid chemicals. Foods containing trans fat have a very long shelf life. They will raise your LDL and lower your HDL cholesterol—the opposite of what you want! Read the ingredients list on all packaged food. It is amazing how many products you will find this in. Beef, lamb, and dairy contain some naturally occurring trans fats, and in moderation that is OK.

Exercise 19 - Food Journaling

We've discussed macro nutrients, whole foods and processed foods. Now is a great time to begin a food journal. Take a look at your earlier mind map for Vitality. Was there something there you wrote about that pertains to your health and food? Did you decide you wanted to become a vegetarian, did you want to give up coffee, was it related to weight loss, do you need to kick your sugar habit but are not sure how much you are eating? By keeping a food journal, you can hold yourself accountable to your goals. It will make you think about everything you are eating and often help you to make a better choice. You will see exactly what you are eating, how much and how often. Keep a journal for 14 days and see if you can connect the dots with what you eat, how foods make you feel and what you may need to change. Use the following guidelines to help you.

Write the following in your journal:

(a) What the foods are and the serving size you consumed. Use the portion size guidelines below to estimate your serving size. Note - not all foods are listed, but this will give you an idea of food types.
(b) The time each food was consumed
(c) How it made you feel right after eating
(d) How you felt 2 hours later
(e) The place or situation you were in during your meal or snack

A closed fist = 1 cup cooked grains, pasta, veggies
Palm of hand = 3 ounces meat, fish, poultry
4 dice = 1-ounce nuts, seeds, raisins
A light bulb = 1-ounce chips, popcorn, pretzels
Your thumb = 1-ounce nuts, butters, hard cheese
Tip of thumb = 1 teaspoon oils, butter, sugars, syrups, mayonnaise

Journaling can be time-consuming. But it is only for 14 days, and the results should give you some insight into how food affects your life both physically and emotionally. For you to be successful, you need to choose a journaling style that works for you and your life. Here are some ideas:

- Using pen and paper and writing everything down the old fashioned way
- Taking photos of your meals and snacks in addition to writing how those meals make you feel
- Creating a spreadsheet that you can access from your phone or on your computer
- Keeping a white board in your kitchen
- Using an app from the App Store to help you record foods. This is a great option, but they do not always have the additional and essential part of recording how food makes you feel, so you may need to add that in somewhere.

When you have completed two weeks of journals, look back over them and decide where you could make some changes. Ask yourself the following questions:

- Was it a whole food?
- Why did I eat that?
- What was going on for me when I ate…?
- Did that food serve me well?

Listen to your gut and see what arises from these questions.

Getting Organized

The key to successful meal planning, grocery shopping, and cooking is getting organized. Dinnertimes seems to be one of the busiest times in people's schedules, more so if you have children at home and find you have a lot of extracurricular activities you have to get them to. If you don't make the time to plan ahead, dinnertime disaster will continue to prevail in your home! You know the kind of disaster I'm talking about, right? You open the fridge at 6 pm and think to yourself, "What am I going to cook?" Nothing jumps out at you, so you either eat a bowl of cereal or order pizza. Sounds familiar, right!

Let's begin with a grocery list. There are many ways to do this. Here are some suggestions:

Type one into a document and itemize the different areas of the store you will buy from such as produce; dairy; meat, poultry & fish; canned goods; crackers, grains and legumes; frozen foods; beverages; bread and cereal; cleaning supplies; toiletries; and baking supplies.

Keep a running list in your kitchen. I tend to use the inside of my kitchen cupboards as notice boards. When a family member sees something run out, ask them to add it to the list.

Stick a chalkboard or dry erase board to your fridge, and add to the list as things run out. Take a photo with your phone, and there's your grocery list.

Use an online app. The following apps work on both android and iOS devices. Cozi—I use this app for the simple calendar, but it also has a grocery list feature. You may also like to try Meal Board. Meal Board helps with grocery lists and menu planning and also offers recipes. If having recipes at your fingertips is essential, try Big Oven—it offers over 350,000 recipes and meal planning advice. Another simple app is Out of Milk, which unites your pantry inventory and a running grocery list on the go.

Menu Planning

I like to plan my meals a month out, but I understand that for some people this can be overwhelming. To begin, pick a day of the week you will commit to meal planning. This may be a weekend if you have more time. Weekends are also an excellent opportunity to look through recipes you may have saved from magazines or cookbooks. If I try out a new recipe from a magazine or a book and it ends up being a keeper, I scan it into the cloud under my recipes folder and then I can view it on my iPad another time. The iPad or your phone is a handy tool to have in the kitchen if you need to follow a recipe from time to time.

Choose to plan either a few meals at a time or a week's worth. I tend to only plan dinners, as usually we eat leftovers for lunch. Sometimes, I will plan special weekend brunches, but not every week. The next thing is to identify if there are any evenings during the week that you know to be busier than others. This may be because you or your spouse is working late or perhaps you have an extra busy night with the kids' schedules. On those nights I either use my crock pot or we eat leftovers from the dinner the night before. If you are using your crock pot, it makes sense to prepare it the night before if you have a rushed morning schedule. You could do this at the same time you are preparing your evening meal or later.

When you have been menu planning for some time, you will be able to rotate through your menus, which is what I do. I keep a paper copy of the week's menus pinned up in the kitchen. You could keep paper copies, use a chalkboard or keep them on your phone—whatever appeals to you. If, like me, you get bored with the rotation and you feel you want to deviate from the plan here and there or you go out to eat, that's fine. Just pick up where you left off the next day.

During the week your meals should be simple, balanced and quick to prepare. Ideally, you want to be able to cook dinner in 20-30 minutes. The weekends are the best time for trying out new dishes that may require a little more time. Think back to the macronutrients we discussed earlier. Eating a balanced meal means it should be made up of all the macronutrients: complex carbohydrates, protein and healthy fats. Below is a typical week's worth of meals I would cook for my family.

- Monday Vegetarian Night - Black bean burgers on a 100% whole wheat bun with sliced avocado, tomato, and lettuce. A side of organic blue corn chips and a green salad.

- Tuesday - Baked wild caught salmon, steamed broccoli, brown rice and a green salad

- Wednesday - Brown rice from the night before, marinated Asian style chicken breast grilled, bok choy and sugar snaps stir fried with garlic, vegetable broth and Brags aminos.

- Thursday - Leftover cooked chicken from last night gets turned into a chicken, vegetable (chop extra vegetables for tomorrow night's dinner) and cannelloni bean soup. Served with grilled cheese sandwiches on 100% whole wheat bread and a green salad.

- Friday - Roasted root vegetables (sweet potatoes, carrots, parsnips), baked cod and a green salad. The leftover root vegetables I usually put in a frittata for brunch. (Prepare the crock pot for tomorrow night.)

- Saturday - Crock pot Mexican chicken or pork, served with all the toppings - sour cream, homemade guacamole and salsa, organic taco shells or soft tacos. Stir fry bell peppers, bok choy, spring onions, tomatoes, garlic, and cilantro.

- Sunday - Marinated grilled steak & vegetable kebabs, quinoa salad, and asparagus. (Mondays are busy, so this is sometimes a leftover meal from Sunday.)

Notice some nights I will use some of the food from the previous evening's meal. Some weeks we will eat leftovers twice and a crock pot meal twice; it depends on my schedule and how much time I will have. You may also notice that we eat a green salad usually 6 days a week, and we eat it after our main meal. We do this because it cleans the palette and can help ward off nighttime snacking and sweet cravings.

More Tips

Whenever you are cooking, get into the habit of cooking double the amount. That way you can cook once and eat two to three more times. You can eat the leftovers during the week or freeze them so you can begin to build up a supply of meals that you can reheat on the evenings you are rushed or don't want to cook.

If you are cooking grains, cook double the amount, allow to cool, and portion out into zip lock bags and freeze. You can then eat them as a side dish or add to soups and stews.

When you are meal planning, think about how you can change each meal into a different dinner. For example, if you cook a pork tenderloin, use the extra one and turn into barbecue pulled pork sandwiches. Or if you make hamburgers, cook some extras for another night. If you decide to have a roast chicken dinner, make two and use the leftovers for chicken tacos, chicken caesar salad, chicken soup, chicken stir fry, etc.

If you are interested in having a morning breakfast smoothie, choose one day a week where you prep and bag up the veggies and fruits and freeze. All you have to do in the morning is add liquid, the bag of goodies and protein powder. I like plant based protein powders such as organic pea, brown rice or hemp.

Eating Clean During Moving (PCS) Season

During PCS season all your good efforts of eating clean whole foods may fly out of the window, but it doesn't have to be that way, even on the long cross-country road trips we military spouses do so often. Here are some tips to eat as clean as possible from the week of pack out to on the go car trips.

- Plan simple crock pot meals for your family during the pack out.
- Feed your packers some healthy nitrate-free deli meat options, whole grain bread, baked chips and fruit, and let them assemble their sub lunches. They will be thankful it's not pizza, and it will be a healthy enough option for you and your family.
- Plan a time a few weeks out and make extra meals at dinnertime with the idea of freezing them for use during pack out week.
- Buy a ready cooked roast chicken from your grocery store deli counter and put it with a quick bag salad or change into chicken wraps.
- Have a cooler in your car with ice packs - use the hotel fridges to re-freeze them when you stop driving for the day.

Or in an emergency fill zip lock bags with ice. Hotels always have ice.
* Pack some paper towels, disposable spoons, and napkins.
* Pack each person a BPA-free, re-usable water bottle that you can fill up during the journey.
* Pack each person a reusable lunch snack bag that you can put snacks into.
* Stop at grocery stores along the way and restock your cooler with healthy snacks such as cheese sticks, fruit, nuts, healthy low sugar granola bars, individual packets of hummus and a box of high fiber crackers or organic chips, bags of carrots, sugar-free apple sauce, organic yogurt and whole grain pretzels.

If you stop for a meal and you are in the middle of nowhere, which happens, and you are limited to fast food restaurants, don't despair. Make the cleanest choice you can. Stay away from the heavy fat foods such as fries and fried foods like burgers and hot dogs. Opt for grilled chicken sandwiches, soups, salads and fruit slices. Drink water, and avoid sodas and sugary juices.

Why Do I Get Food Cravings?

You know the deal, the chips and dip are calling your name; you crave Ben and Jerry's ice cream at ten o'clock at night, you cannot make it through the afternoon without a Starbucks "dessert coffee drink" or chocolate chip cookies haunt your dreams! We have all experienced some kind of craving at some time. But what people ask me is: Why? Why do I crave sugar, alcohol, salty foods or spicy foods?

We are preconditioned to believe if we crave foods and we give in to them that we are weak willed. We reprimand ourselves often in a mean tone; we belittle ourselves and emotionally beat ourselves up over our food craving behaviors. This is not OK; please stop doing this! You would never talk to your friend in such a disrespectful way if they came to you and expressed their darkest secret, their peanut butter cup addiction! You surely wouldn't have many friends if you did! So, to keep on your good side, be kind—that's the first step.

The second is to figure out why you are having such cravings. Keeping your food journal will help with this. You may begin to see a pattern of when you crave certain foods and why. Be sure to include all cravings in your food journal. Note when they happened, what you had just eaten, and the situation/mood you were in at that time.

Cravings can be emotional or physical. Physical cravings are your body's way of telling you that something in your body is out of balance. You may be deficient in certain micro and macro nutrients. You may experience cravings because you need more fat or lean protein in your diet. You could be low on minerals or a particular vitamin. I often see clients who have developed a taste for vinegary, sour flavors or extreme salty foods. Sometimes a certain consistency of foods such as crunchy are craved. These are usually associated with nutritional deficiencies. It is not uncommon in the summer months to crave foods that are cooling to the body like salads, ice cream, milkshakes, fruits or raw foods. In the winter months, you may have experienced cravings for hot and warming foods such as heavy stews, soups, fatty meats or casseroles. This is your body's way of telling you what it needs for that particular season to help you produce adequate energy and stay healthy.

    One of the most common causes of cravings is caused by dehydration. That's why we so often hear that we should drink a glass of water and wait 10 minutes before we give in to a craving. This is a great idea and one which I recommend. Other reasons for such imbalances are hormonal such as pregnancy, peri menopause, menopause, and PMS. Another trick to helping reduce cravings is to use a tongue scraper. You can buy them at your local pharmacy or grocery store. You scrape your tongue daily or at the time of the craving. Some clients like to brush their teeth after a meal to prevent them from craving sweet desserts or alcohol. Brushing your teeth sends a signal to your brain that you are finished eating for the day.

The additional information that cravings are telling us is that there is an emotional connection. You may eat a healthy diet but still crave certain foods. This is when you need to take a deeper look at what is going on for you. Look at your 5 Power mind maps that you made in the early exercise in this book: ambition, play, vitality, connection, and inner peace. Are there a lot of gaps in your life where you feel you are not living an intentional life? Do you feel there is something missing in these areas? When we feel dissatisfied with our lives, we crave. We crave all kinds of things from physical affection, to peace and quiet, to fun and adventure. We may feel stressed, insecure, overwhelmed or bored. Listen to your gut. What is it telling you at that very moment you crave a certain food? Listen and ask again. Then decide how you will resolve the craving. Sure you can eat a brownie and get a temporary quick fix, but unfortunately that is only the short answer. You must delve deeper. If I am ever feeling sad or stressed, I crave foods from my childhood like fish and chips or a vanilla slice, which is a yummy custard and jam filled pastry.

Even your health coach doesn't crave broccoli or a salad in that situation; no one is perfect! You may have noticed you crave foods from your childhood. Perhaps when you were a child you ate that particular food on a special occasion. It may have been a treat, or you may associate the food you crave with a special person in your family. Maybe you have fond memories of baking with your grandma? Analyze your situation, and get some answers. Ask yourself whether you are craving food due to a physical imbalance or if there is an emotional connection.

Client Story

I worked with a client who was addicted to sugar. Her craving was so intense that she drank 2 cups of sugar a day in her homemade iced tea so that she could function and get through her busy day with her work and young children. Her cravings were due to both nutritional and emotional deficiencies in her life. First, we worked on the nutritional part of gaining back better balance with the food she was taking in. We got her to a place where she was eating high-quality foods throughout the day. Then using the tools I suggested, together we slowly began to tackle weaning her off her sugar addiction. This took some time. Giving up such a strong sugar addiction is not easy. Some scientists say it is as hard as giving up crack cocaine. The side effects from giving up sugar are not fun; there are headaches and mood swings to name a couple. Working on my client's nutritional deficiencies first was essential. By bringing her body back into homeostasis, she then had the physical stamina to address the emotional baggage she was carrying around with her. I am happy to say she conquered all and continued to live a happy and healthy life without the need for her sugar crutch.

The Importance of Sleep - Get some Zzz's

Are you someone who burns the candle at both ends? Do you stay up late and get up early regularly? Or do you toss and turn all night long like a fish out of water? If this sounds familiar, you are hurting your health. My clients more often than not overlook their need for quality sleep. They have cornered their beliefs into thinking if they stay up late they will be able to catch up on home chores or get a head start on the next day's work projects. They think they are productive, but in fact they are not. They are draining their battery until one day that battery is 'dead', and they wake up sick. Our bodies are not designed to go, go, go 24/7! Did you know that not getting enough sleep can contribute to a thicker waistline? That's because sleep deprivation leads to an imbalance in your blood sugar levels, making you feel hungrier. Without addressing your sleep, you are putting yourself at risk for insulin resistance, which can lead to type 2 diabetes, a depressed immune function, mood swings, and a lower life expectancy. We need rest, relaxation, exercise, play, and sleep. Most adults require 7-8 hours of sleep every night. I know some of you can survive on less, but do you want to survive or thrive? People who have this mindset call themselves night owls. If you are a night owl, you still need 7-8 hours of sleep, but my guess is you may be getting 6 hours or less. The next day, you drag yourself out of bed and coax your body with caffeine to prepare you for the day ahead. Now ask yourself: Was it worth staying up? How could you be feeling right now if you'd gone to bed earlier? Most of us have been in this situation at some point in our lives. Doing this here and there is OK, but making this a regular habit is not healthy for you, your body or your relationship with your sleeping buddy! Everything is affected by staying up too late. Ideally, you need to set yourself a bedtime routine, just like the one you had as a child. Remember those days; it would begin with your mom or dad running you a warm bath followed by a hot drink and a snack and then a bedtime story. It was relaxing and comforting, wasn't it? So what happened? Why are you now on social media, watching horrifying stories on the news, cleaning or doing that last load of laundry? We have to change your routine to encourage a more restful night's sleep.

Bedtime Tips

- Begin by turning off all electronics about 1 hour before you intend to go to sleep. The blue light from iPads, computer screens, and televisions all impact your melatonin levels.
- Melatonin is a hormone that your body makes naturally, and it helps us to get a restful night's sleep. As we age we lose melatonin. You may wish to discuss supplementation with your doctor.
- Write your concerns down in a notebook so that they do not weigh on your mind before bed.
- Remove the television from your bedroom. Your bed should be a place for romantic liaisons with your spouse and sleep.
- Drink a relaxing herbal tea such as lavender, chamomile or one of the Yogi brand nighttime teas.
- Take a warm bath. Try adding essential oils that are calming such as lavender or Epsom salts and bicarbonate of soda. The magnesium will help you relax.
- Do not eat a heavy meal right before bed. Try to eat dinner 2-3 hours before going to bed.

- Do not exercise vigorously after dinner. An evening stroll or gentle yoga is fine, but hard workouts rev up your energy systems.
- Avoid alcohol and caffeine—you will sleep much deeper without your body trying to work these through your liver.

Get your body into a schedule. Go to sleep and wake up at the same time every day, even on the weekends if you can. Ideally, I would like to see you asleep no later than 10 PM. If you go to sleep later than this, it puts your body into a different circadian rhythm. Your circadian rhythm is the natural 24-hour cycle that your body follows. It gives you the appropriate energy levels throughout the day and allows you to feel sleepy at the right time. It gets disrupted when you have no set bedtime routine like if you are a night shift worker or you experienced jet lag.

It would be nice if we could go to sleep when it's dark and wake naturally when it is light out and without the need for an alarm, but this is not possible for most people. The next best thing is to establish and commit to a bedtime routine.

Get Active!

Where are you at with exercise? You may be a gung ho athlete type or an "I'll start next week" procrastination exerciser! Look on your Vitality mind map. What did you write down for exercise goals? What has prevented you from achieving these goals in the past? Were they overwhelming, unrealistic, too time consuming or not fun? The most important piece of advice I will offer you is only to choose an exercise that you will enjoy participating in. If you hate running or loathe spin class, why would you set that as a realistic goal? Life is too short to do things you don't enjoy! When you find a type of exercise you enjoy, you will be more likely to commit to it several times a week. As a certified personal trainer and Pilates instructor, I know there are some forms of exercise that I would love all my clients to be doing regularly. But I also respect that they may not find them to be enjoyable. At the end of the day we just need to move our bodies, so we need to do whatever it takes to accomplish that. You may have heard the words 'sitting is the new smoking.' The increased number of hours you spend sitting can up your risk for heart-related diseases, type 2 diabetes, and obesity. That's why now we see so many people using step counting devices such as apps on iPhones to watches, stand up desks, and in some work places you'll even see stretching charts or posters encouraging workers to get up and move.

What Should I Do, When Should I Do it and Why?

Clients always ask me what the best type of exercise they should do is and how often should they do it, and I always give them the same answer—the path that you will stick with! Ideally, you need to work out most days of the week, so six days a week with a day of rest. Some of you may need two days of rest. You should also consider the intensity of those workouts. If you exercise six times per week, you wouldn't want every week to be a high-intensity week or a low-intensity week. You need to vary the exercises and the intensity and incorporate complementary exercise modalities such as yoga or Pilates to balance out your workouts. Just as you cannot justify yoga or Pilates to give you heart pounding cardio workout, you cannot expect running to work your muscles in the same way a weight training program would. If you enjoy exercise, creating a program for yourself that incorporates variety and intensity will be fun. On the other hand, if you are not an exercise fanatic, you may be wondering if walking alone and some gentle stretching is enough. The answer is yes that would be OK as long as your expectations of what you will achieve from your program are realistic. If you want sculpted arms, for example, and lean, muscular legs, walking alone won't cut it—sorry to bear the bad news! But if you are looking just to move your body and improve your existing sedentary life, then that is what you will get. I'm a health nut and have always loved to workout. However, I do understand that this is not everyone's priority. What is good for one person is another's poison! You need to find what you love and stick with it, and if your exercise program does not involve resistance training, I'm going to preach that over and over again. Please for the love of your skeleton add some in! Let's talk about your options and come up with a way to make exercise a part of your life, not something that overtakes your life.

Get a Healthy Heart

Any exercise that raises your heart rate is a form of cardiovascular exercise. Cardio vascular exercise is important; it gets your heart rate up, which helps to improve oxygen consumption. Cardio can help you to lose weight or maintain weight, lower your blood pressure and your resting heart rate, improve heart health, increase your strength and endurance, and make everyday living activities easier.

There are tons of ways to get cardio workouts into your day. If you live on a base, you will no doubt have access to a fitness facility that has a whole host of exercise machines such as stationary bikes, treadmills, stair masters, elliptical trainers and a swimming pool. If you are someone who prefers to work out in this environment, I would suggest you try out all the machines and see which you enjoy. You may also try out some of the group exercise classes. If you are new to exercise and have not been doing anything for quite some time, please begin slowly. You may start out with 15 minutes on a piece of cardio equipment and gradually over the following weeks increase your time to the length of your desired workout. If you are trying a class for the first time, let the instructor know that you have been sedentary and that you may need to work at a slower pace and possibly shorten your time in class until you can complete the whole workout.

If the gym scene makes you cringe and you know you are more of an outdoor person, look at the options based on where you live. Are there any good walking/running trails or hikes you could try? Do you live near the ocean or a lake you could swim in? Do you want to ride a bike or cross country ski, go rollerblading or skateboarding? Walking is a very popular outdoor exercise program because it is free and you can do it anywhere. But don't limit yourself to only walking. Check out meetup.com for outdoor group exercise classes. They range from cardio classes like high-intensity training to group bike rides and runs to mind-body modalities. Seek and you shall find!

    Some people like to work out in the comfort of their own homes. You may do this while your kids are still sleeping or just because it is more convenient than driving to the gym or dealing with incremental weather. You have many options at home. You may have a piece of exercise equipment that you have been using as a clothes horse—time to clean it up and get on it! Or you may enjoy downloading YouTube workouts or subscribing to one of the many popular online fitness programs. You can even keep it as simple as dancing in your house! I have many clients who hate to exercise but love to dance; some say Zumba needs too much coordination, so I recommend they just put on their iPod and dance! There's something special about dancing; it makes you feel happy and relaxed, and you forget you are exerting yourself. You may feel a little bit silly at first, but stick with it and reap the benefits. If you live in a home that has a staircase, you have your own built in stair master. Working intervals on your stairs in combination with other moves will burn calories and keep you fit—more on this later.

Pumping Iron!

This is truly your fountain of youth right here at its best! Resistance training is good for the young and old alike and everyone in between. If you want to add some pep to your step, add resistance training to your life and never stop. That's right; I said never stop! Your wellness weapon of youth is strength training. As we age, we begin to lose bone density and muscle mass. Unless we tax these systems, we gradually wither away and what's left is extra fat and saggy skin! Yikes, sounds depressing, right? After age forty we lose 0.3 to 0.5 percent of our bone mass. That's about 1% every year. In this scenario, we begin to look old, withered, weak and bent over; we lose our balance, fall and break a hip, and end up never fully recovering. For some of you, this may seem a long way down the road, especially if you are only in your 20's and 30's. But for those of you in your 40's, 50's, and 60's plus, the race against time is real. Muscle cells are affected as we age. The plump, juicy muscles that you have in your younger years begin to deteriorate from about age forty years on. They deteriorate even when you are young if you do not tax the system; it just happens at a slower rate. If you snooze you lose! When we lose muscle mass, our metabolism slows down, and we end up with a higher body fat percentage, and this leads to weight gain. Naturally, your body as you age will change, and it will always look different than the days of your youth. But how you function is key to your health and vitality. When you watch a toddler playing, they move their bodies in all planes of motion. They go from standing to sitting to crawling and rolling around from tummy to back, and then they will repeat this pattern over and over again. Can you emulate a toddler at play? That should be our goal. You are as young as you can play and move. I have trained people in their 20's and 30's who cannot get down on the floor to play with their kids to grandparents who could outrun their children. Age is just a number if you feel fit and healthy. If you lift weights that tax your system, you will be able to maintain your strong, lean muscles, tendons, bones, and ligaments. You will have a sexy, powerful body for the age you are at, and that will give you confidence. Notice I said for the age you are at. Be realistic—at 40 or 50 you will not look like you did at 20 or even 30. Grow old gracefully with strength, fitness and flexibility.

Do I Need to Contort Myself into a Pretzel Shape?

Ahhh stretching—the dessert after exercise! Yes, you need to work on your flexibility, but no you do not need to become a master Iyengar Yogi! I encourage you to work on your range of motion because it will help you to keep feeling young and injury free. Making time to stretch needs to fit into your schedule. You may have a short amount of time to work out in the morning, and your flexibility training may come later in the day. For example, when you're listening to your kids read in the evening or if you are sitting on the floor playing with your children. You may do a series of stretches throughout the day, making time to get up from your desk and move. Or you may be someone who is committed to a short yoga practice before bed. Whenever and wherever you can fit in your flexibility program is great. Just make sure you are doing something daily. You can use Dyna bands, yoga blocks and straps to assist you.

You may also like to purchase a foam roller or a massage stick for self myo fascial release to help get all those little knots out of your muscles. It won't be as much fun as visiting your massage therapist, but it will bring you some relief from worked muscles and DOMS delayed onset muscle soreness. Fascia is a combination of hard and soft collagen fibers that join the body together. It's an intricate web that is closely connected to the nervous system, and they talk to each other to help the body function optimally. Myo fascial release techniques are an essential part of your flexibility routine.

    We have identified the three exercise systems: flexibility, cardiovascular exercise and resistance training exercises. Aerobic exercise will help your heart stay healthy and strong, and functional weight training and flexibility training will give you quality of life, making your activities of everyday living easier. No matter what your age, ideally you need to begin a training program that incorporates all of these areas and one that is appropriate for your level of fitness. Take your time to allow your joints and muscles time to adapt to the stresses you will place on them so that you can prevent injury.

Exercise 20 - Vitality Goals

Identify your training goals on your Vitality mind map. Now decide on some action steps to make those goals a reality:

- How much time realistically can you devote to exercising? Be very honest here. This is key to your success.
- How many times per week?
- What days of the week will you do it?
- What will you do on each of those days?
- Where will you do it? Who with?
- What will you do?

Mark all this on your calendar, ensure you will get enough sleep and rest to make this happen, and fuel your body with clean whole foods so that you get optimal results.

More Tips for Getting It Done, No Excuses!

Getting an accountability partner is a great idea if you know you are not likely to show up on your own. This is an excellent way to build friendships with people in your community. Post on your community Facebook page that you are looking for someone to keep you honest. You will be inundated with takers.

If going to the on base fitness center is not an option for you due to lack of child care or just the simple fact you do not enjoy the gym environment, consider trading off with other friends. You can still work out on the days you have your friends' kids if you choose to do something at home. If the kids are old enough to watch a little TV show for 30 minutes, that's your workout time. You can put on your iPod and be in the same room and get a workout in. It's not as ideal as getting away and having time alone, but it is doable and sometimes the only option. Once again this is a chance to practice flexibility and acceptance.

Working out off base is a great idea if the facility offers reasonable rates and they have daycare. This was something I did when my kids were babies and toddlers. It was my sanity saver! YMCA's can be a good option for this. You can put toddlers and preschoolers into clubs and activities and get your workout in while they are busy having their fun.

Working out while your kid's asleep. If you can wake up early enough and dedicate some time in the morning, this is an ideal way to start your day. No need for daycare or having to rely on anyone else. This is a good option if you work outside of the home. Note that you must be in bed on time to make this happen. You don't necessarily need to do this daily. You could mix it up with shared babysitting with your friends or evening workouts when your spouse comes home. Think about how to make it work best for you, knowing yourself and your daily habits.

Start your own club. If there is a group of spouses with or without children wanting to work out, begin a walking or running club. Even on those rainy, snowy, cold days hold each other accountable by having another option such as utilizing the base community center, taking turns in each other's home and so on. Get creative, and look into all your options.

Family workouts can be fun if your kids are either old enough to ride a bike or run/walk alongside or patient enough sit in a jogging stroller. It's ideal if you can work out near a playground that will keep your kids entertained. You may take some resistance bands or a TRX system to use while they play. Working out with your spouse and kids is a team effort and good motivation. The weekends or evening will more than likely be a time to try this.

If it is financially feasible, pay a babysitter or check into drop-in childcare at your child development center and use that time for exercise. Although some base gyms today do offer a family area where the kids can play, and you have enough exercise equipment to get in your own workout. I've used this option over the years.

Find a great novel to listen to or download a TV show on your iPad, but only allow yourself to listen to it while you are moving your body such as walking, running, riding a stationary bike, or lifting weights in the yard at home.

Maybe you can trade up services. Do you know a personal trainer or Pilates Instructor willing to trade services? Say they train you in return for a home cooked meal once a week or free childcare? Get creative, be flexible and think outside the box.

Remember, I want you to be successful. If you have been a couch potato for some time, setting yourself an unrealistic goal of running daily for 30 minutes isn't going to happen. Either you will get hurt or fail to show up. Start easy and build up from there. You have to work on your physical strength and endurance as well as your emotional endurance. To make something become a habit, it needs to be repeated a minimum of 35 times or more!

Home Workout Equipment - What Toys You Need!

Having some basic pieces of equipment at home is a great idea, even if you work out in the gym. Having things at home you can do is helpful if something comes up such as a sick kid or a busier than usual schedule and you cannot make it to the gym that day. Perhaps you would like to have a combination of working out at home and the gym, which is what I like to do.

Basic Home Purchases

- An exercise ball
- A set of dumbbells or the type that is one piece that you can adjust to create different weights
- A jump rope
- Varying resistance bands and a door loop to attach them to your door
- An exercise mat
- A medicine ball

Many stores in the mall and online sell these types of items. Shop around for the best deals.

Other Things to Consider, Nice to Have But Not Necessary

- A step box - you may find one at a yard sale or on Craigslist
- A Bosu Ball
- A piece of cardiovascular equipment like a treadmill or elliptical trainer, or if you have a bike, a bike trainer you can put your bike on
- TRX - the suspension training equipment

What Types of Workouts Should I do?

This question is unique to you and the goals you came up with based on time and interest. But in saying that, every workout program should consist of the basics: cardio, strength and flexibility training that we talked about earlier. Here are some popular options:

H.I.T.

High-Intensity Training is a great time-saving tool and an incredible workout. You can do this at the gym in a class environment or at home using an online website or a video you may have downloaded. You could hire a personal trainer if this is affordable. HIT usually involves both cardiovascular and resistance training moves over a period that is broken down into intervals. It maximizes your time and works the major muscle groups to keep them firing and building strength, power, and endurance. This is a great option if you are short on time.

Functional Resistance Training Programs

Working out with weights can be performed in hundreds of ways, again dependent upon your goals. You can do low weights with high repetitions or the reverse, heavy weights with low repetitions; both will give different results. You can work your whole body in one session or split the body into muscle groups and work them over a series of days. You can use machines, free weights, resistance bands, TRX systems or a combination of all of the above. The moves you perform should be functional. Functional exercises are moments that will help your body to accomplish everyday living activities with ease. When you train your body with functional moves, you are using the biomechanics of the body in the same way you do in daily living, using multi-joint and multi-planar planes moves. If you are new to this type of exercise, check in as some fitness centers will offer a complimentary training session with a personal trainer. They will guide you through a basic program. You can purchase a couple of sessions to get a basic program started or try a class so you get some ideas of the moves you can perform. You can also find hundreds of online options today that can help you to be successful.

Body Weight Training

This is a cheap way to work out using only your body weight, and you can do it anywhere indoors or out. It is a workout that targets the major muscle groups. You may be doing things such as push-ups, pull-ups, squats, lunges, dips, planks and so much more. Body weight exercises can be done in combination with cardiovascular drills such as jumping rope, jumping jacks, burpees, mountain climbers and all the things you will do in a HIT class. There are lots of options to help you get started such as YouTube videos, online virtual gym memberships, and hiring a trainer. Hiring a personal trainer is a great option for people who need the accountability. A coach can also ensure that you stay on track for your target goals and prevent you from plateauing.

Group Exercise

There are so many options to try today that I cannot list all the varieties of group exercise classes out there. Group exercise classes are done in parks, recreation centers, fitness facilities, church halls, schools and so on. They vary from pure cardio classes such as spin classes to running and cycling clubs. There are mind-body classes available to you such as Pilates, yoga and tai chi. You may try a Zumba dance party class, a rock climbing challenge or a resistance training sculpting class. The classes can be done on land, in water, on a piece of exercise equipment, a bike or on your own two feet! Endless amounts of fun await you. Try the ones that appeal to you.

PCS Season Workouts - No Excuses!

If you have some simple pieces of exercise equipment that travel light, don't let the packers pack them. I recommend you take them with you in your suitcase so that you can stay true to your goals during your move. Resistance bands, a jump rope, and a TRX are all good choices, possibly a stability ball and a ball pump too. Most hotels have some kind of exercise equipment that you can use. Even if you have no equipment, you can still get outside and work out while on the road with a quick walk or run followed by some body weight exercises. I've even put on my iPod, let the kids play on their iPads or watch TV, and got in some body weight moves in the hotel room followed by some Pilates. Whatever time and space you have, just move your body! It may not be your usual workout, but it will be enough to keep you motivated, and it will help release some stress.

Safety Tips for Success

Whichever type of exercise workout you choose, please remember to stay hydrated even if you are working out in a cold climate. You need to drink plenty of water before, during and after your workout. If you live in a hot climate and you are working out outdoors, or if your workout is longer than two hours at a high intensity, you should consider drinking a sports drink. Sports drinks will replace your electrolytes. A couple of my favorites are Osmo and Accelerade. I stay away from some drinks due to their high sugar content. Some people prefer to take simple electrolyte capsules with water. Whichever works best for your body is what you need to go with. **Remember - Sports drinks are sugars - don't drink them unless you're sweating hard for more than two hours. Avoid the unneeded calories!**

- Wear sunscreen and a hat if you are training outdoors
- Take a snack along with you in case you experience yourself bonking. Bonking is the term used when a person's glycogen, their blood sugar level, drops and they hit a wall. In this situation, you need a simple carbohydrate to help you. This could be a banana, a tangerine or

some Shot Blocks or Goo. The latter two are found in sports stores; they are fast-acting glucose food sources that are digested quickly.
* Take your phone, identification and some cash—you never know what situation may arise. Having those three things is key.
* Check your running shoes to make sure they are in good shape and not worn out to prevent injury.
* If you are working out alone, stay alert. If it's dark out, stick with well-lit parks and streets and always be sure to tell someone where you are going and when you will be home; this includes the babysitter, a friend, a neighbor or spouse.

References:

http://healthyeating.sfgate.com/primary-role-protein-diet-3403.html

http://medicine.tufts.edu/Education/Academic-Departments/Clinical-Departments/Public-Health-and-Community-Medicine/Nutrition-and-Infection-Unit/Research/Nutrition-and-Health-Topics/Building-a-High-Quality-Diet

https://draxe.com/the-dangers-of-farmed-fish/

https://www.ncbi.nlm.nih.gov/pmc/articles/PMC1552029/

http://www.livestrong.com/article/420546-the-health-benefits-of-complex-carbohydrates-and-diet/

http://www.saragottfriedmd.com/dial-in-the-carbs-choosing-the-right-dose-for-you-in-3-easy-steps/

Closing

After reading this book, how do you now feel about your military life? The military lifestyle is filled with many exciting experiences and opportunities that are unique to military families' lives, if you stay open-minded. Has reading this book awakened a sense of curiosity in you or a new sense of adventure? Did it help you clarify your thoughts and feelings and put some things into perspective? Can you place your hand on your heart and say *yes* to the changes you will continue to face with this military lifestyle? I hope you have a renewed sense of self-confidence to go out and get what you want.

Thank you for taking the time to read my book and complete the exercises. May I suggest you read it a second time, picking and choosing the chapters where you need the most support. Work on your *5 Power Area* mind maps for these particular areas that are unique to your needs today, and come up with your action plans so that you can get the life you want. Always consider your *4 Cornerstones of Life* with everything you tackle. Remember, you are a military spouse who *Holds Down The Fort* every day. Be proud of that and stand tall!

You are amazing, strong, resilient and capable of anything if you want it enough and are creative enough in your approach.

My Hope for You

*I hope you never settle for second best.
I hope you dare to dream and make those dreams a reality.
I hope you see your life as an advantage and not a disadvantage.
I hope you live your life with passion.
I hope you seek help and never feel lost.
I hope you find a friend.
I hope you find peace in times of crazy adventures.
I hope you feel supported.
I hope you feel worthy.
I hope you love your life.
I hope you feel proud of who you are and remember you are never alone…*

My support and care across the miles we share.

Warmly,

Navenka

Testimonies

Navenka is a health coach who met me on day one with energy and professionalism, but with warmth and a personal touch that made meeting with her something I looked forward to. Coming with a wealth of practical health knowledge each session, she gave appropriate tools and tips for day to day living that could improve my daily nutritional routines. She took the time to listen to my unique needs and tailor a program to help me take small steps towards my personal health goals. After our three month program, I felt turned in a new direction with my life dreams and my health goals and propelled toward my goals in a way I knew I could continue.

Mom, Military Spouse

I can't say enough about how much I value Navenka; she is my secret wellness weapon! I approached Navenka after reaching a level of back pain that was impacting my ability to function in both my professional and personal lives. Navenka quickly assessed my situation and recommended wellness coaching, personal training, and Pilates. She integrated her services with the care that I was receiving from my primary care provider, chiropractor, and physical therapist. After three months, the result is that I am largely pain-free, have lost inches, have more energy, feel both calmer and stronger. I highly recommend Navenka's services to anyone who is willing to make changes in their life to be healthier and more fit. Navenka has a unique ability to look at you as a whole person which is really the only way to make lasting change.

Naval Officer and Mom

From the very first meeting which was done on Google Hangouts, an app that allows you to see each other, I WAS HOOKED!! Navenka's concern and commitment to ME were unbelievable. She listened as I explained regardless of counting calories or exercise that I was actually gaining weight and that at the end of the day I was always tired.
To say that Navenka has changed my life is an understatement!! I have lost 23 lbs. and 7-3/4 inches overall. I have never felt better! I loved the way she always kept me in check with myself and taught me that my weight wasn't only about what I was putting in my mouth but my actual lifestyle!

Who would have guessed that adding a simple 2 hours (or sometimes 3!!!) of sleep a night could be such a positive change in your life? Navenka's holistic approach to my health and wellness has improved my energy level and created such a happy, healthy life for me.

If you had told me a year ago that one person could change your life in such a dramatic way, I would have been the first person to say it wouldn't happen. I can easily say that Navenka has become a part of my life and that I'm dreading the sessions ending and will be signing up for future ones! I am a new person; not in just that my clothes fit better but as an overall individual!

I strongly recommend contacting Navenka for an initial consultation to see how she can help you. Don't wait any longer to get in control of YOU and your life.

Empty Nester

Reviews

"As a former military member and current military spouse, I wholeheartedly agree with Navenka's holistic approach to achieving a fulfilled life. I personally practice many of her recommendations and absolutely recommend that you do too! Understanding the difference between merely existing and living with a purpose has been a real eye-opener for me. The reality is that the life of a military spouse: running the household, caring for the children, trying to have a career, etc., is a constant challenge. In my experience, being the spouse is often more stressful than being the service member. But fear not, these challenges can be overcome! Reading this book and applying its information is your first step in learning how to live a meaningful, satisfying life. I strongly recommend all military spouses read this book!"

John E

"If you are disciplined enough to follow Navenka's principles in this book, then you will be on a good start to a healthy life journey. "

Air Force spouse of 22 years

This book was well written and enjoyable. I am a military dependent and could relate to the author and many of the testimonies in this book. I liked that Navenka gave exercises to bring home the point she was making in the various chapters. She stressed that people need both primary food and secondary food to feel complete. I found this insightful.

If you are feeling on the verge of making changes in your life and need an extra push then this is the book for you. Mrs Gabrielson has years of experience assisting individuals as a Health Coach and reading what she has learned has been eye opening for me. I may even look at getting a Health Coach to assist me after reading this book.

Naddett S Navy Spouse of 30 years

"Holding Down the Fort perfectly summarizes the demands on military spouses and empowers them to take control of their situation. Navenka Gabrielson's casual, yet gut checking questions challenge spouses to evaluate their personal priorities and find their own success. Her acknowledgement of the struggles with identity and purpose are perfectly articulated. The integral mind, soul and body approach targets the 4 Cornerstones and 5 Power Areas, enabling spouses to seek peace and fulfillment regardless of duty station or deployment cycle and puts them in control, not the detailer. Holding Down the Fort is an important resource for all spouses, young and old, as a guide on how to get the best out of any situation and grow into your best self."

Navy Spouse

About The Author

Navenka Gabrielson grew up in the humble industrial region of Lancashire, Northern England. With no idea of what lay ahead, she married a naval officer in the U.S. Navy. Twenty years later, Navenka and her family have lived all over the United States, including both coasts, the Midwest, Hawaii, and now Southeast Asia, surviving well over a dozen moves with two kids, dogs, fish and countless adventures.

Navenka's passion helps people live happy, healthy lives, balancing nutrition, exercise, and lifestyle. She founded Body Harmony, helping others through her skills as a nationally-certified Health and Lifestyle Coach, Personal Trainer and Pilates instructor. Her non-judgmental listening style helps military spouses, service members, and government civilians alike, both locally and worldwide. Navenka presents speaking engagements both online and locally on health, wellness, and mindful living.

Navenka discovered a true passion for life along the way - she learned to swim, ride a bike, and the joys of life outside her comfort zone. She also enjoys time outdoors with her family, traveling, hiking, biking, or just relaxing. She is a keen potter who enjoys the challenge of throwing ceramics on a potter's wheel.

To learn more, please visit her website at bodyharmonyonline.com and consider registering for a complimentary health coaching session and her email newsletter.